Cambridge Elements ≡

Elements in Global China
edited by
Ching Kwan Lee
University of California–Los Angeles

THE HONG KONG–CHINA NEXUS

A Brief History

John M. Carroll
University of Hong Kong

CAMBRIDGE
UNIVERSITY PRESS

CAMBRIDGE
UNIVERSITY PRESS

University Printing House, Cambridge CB2 8BS, United Kingdom

One Liberty Plaza, 20th Floor, New York, NY 10006, USA

477 Williamstown Road, Port Melbourne, VIC 3207, Australia

314–321, 3rd Floor, Plot 3, Splendor Forum, Jasola District Centre,
New Delhi – 110025, India

103 Penang Road, #05–06/07, Visioncrest Commercial, Singapore 238467

Cambridge University Press is part of the University of Cambridge.

It furthers the University's mission by disseminating knowledge in the pursuit of
education, learning, and research at the highest international levels of excellence.

www.cambridge.org
Information on this title: www.cambridge.org/9781108789776
DOI: 10.1017/9781108893275

First published 2022

A catalogue record for this publication is available from the British Library.

ISBN 978-1-108-78977-6 Paperback
ISSN 2632-7341 (online)
ISSN 2632-7333 (print)

The Hong Kong–China Nexus

A Brief History

Elements in Global China

DOI: 10.1017/9781108893275
First published online: March 2022

John M. Carroll
University of Hong Kong

Author for correspondence: John M. Carroll, jcarroll@hku.hk

Abstract: The Occupy Central/Umbrella Movement of 2014 and the anti-extradition protests of 2019 revealed how much Hong Kong's relationship with mainland China has deteriorated since the former British colony returned to Chinese sovereignty in July 1997. With mutual distrust and suspicion at an all-time high, many Hong Kong people have become increasingly hostile toward the Chinese government and the mainland in general, identifying themselves as Hongkongers rather than as Chinese. Yet, as John Carroll shows, for more than 150 years, colonial Hong Kong and China not only coexisted with but benefited each other, even during the anti-imperialist campaigns of the Republican and Communist eras. The porous boundary between Hong Kong and China enabled the two to use each other economically, politically, socially, and culturally. The Hong Kong–China nexus, although firmly embedded in global dynamics of colonialism, Cold War politics, and capitalist expansion, defies many common assumptions about nationalism, colonialism, and decolonization.

Keywords: Hong Kong, China, Colonialism, Nationalism, Decolonization, Postcolonialism

ISBNs: 9781108789776 (PB), 9781108893275 (OC)
ISSNs: 2632-7341 (online), 2632-7333 (print)

Contents

Figure F Hong Kong and vicinity, 1998 (Library of Congress
Geography and Map Division)

1 Introducing the Nexus

The return of Hong Kong to Chinese sovereignty on July 1, 1997, was a diplomatic, moral, and psychological victory for China. It ended the humiliating "unequal treaties" that had begun in January 1841 with the cession of Hong Kong Island to Britain during the Opium War (1839–1842). Overnight, this former British colony became the first Special Administrative Region (SAR) of the People's Republic of China (PRC). It was followed two years later by Macau, which had been occupied by the Portuguese in the mid-1500s. In the two-plus decades since, the Chinese government has frequently reminded Hong Kong (and the world) how much its continued prosperity – indeed, its very survival – depend on Beijing's support and goodwill.

Meanwhile, since 1997 but especially over the past few years, many Hong Kong people have become increasingly hostile toward the Chinese government and the mainland in general, identifying as Hong Kong people – Hongkongese or Hongkongers (*Heunggongyahn*) – rather than as Chinese. This form of self-identification had emerged much earlier. But it became even more widespread as Hong Kong became further integrated with mainland China. The annual protest march on July 1, for example, quickly became an occasion to express dissatisfaction with the Hong Kong and Chinese governments. In 1998, marchers protested against President Jiang Zemin's visit. In 1999, activists shouting "Democracy for China" interrupted Vice President Hu Jintao's speech at the unveiling ceremony for a monument commemorating Hong Kong's reunification with China. In 2004, hundreds of thousands protested the Chinese government's decision to prohibit general elections in the SAR.

During the 2012 march, the largest in almost one decade, the participants voiced their usual demands and complaints: universal suffrage for Hong Kong and too much interference from Beijing. And a small but noticeable number of marchers began to wave the British and former Hong Kong colonial flags. These actions stirred further controversy, especially when an internet movement called for Hong Kong to become an independent state. (In the entire history of colonial Hong Kong, no one had ever issued such a demand, nor was there a single attempt to overthrow the government or return to Chinese sovereignty.) In October, protesters waved British and colonial Hong Kong flags in front of the Chinese government's liaison office, chanting slogans such as "We Are Hongkongers, Not Chinese." Condemning such actions, Lu Ping, the former head of the Chinese State Council's Hong Kong and Macau Affairs Office, dismissed advocates for independence as "sheer morons." Without support from the mainland, he insisted, Hong Kong would become a "dead city." During the 2013 march, a new slogan appeared: "Chinese Colonists Get Out."

Since then, relations between Hong Kong and mainland China have become even worse. In 2015, concerns about the SAR's autonomy intensified when five booksellers connected to a local shop selling books banned in the mainland went missing and mysteriously appeared across the border. In January 2017, a Chinese-Canadian billionaire known for managing assets for the families of prominent Chinese leaders vanished from his hotel, leaving many to believe that he too had been snatched by mainland agents. The main theme for the July march was "One Country, Two Systems: A Lie for Twenty Years." But that year's march included two new slogans: "Hong Kong Independence" and "Hong Kong Is Not China." According to a survey in December 2019, only 11 percent of the respondents considered themselves Chinese – the lowest level since 1997. The national security law passed on June 30, 2020, during the COVID-19 pandemic and following months of protest and social unrest in 2019, has only further inflamed these long-simmering tensions. It has convinced many Hong Kong people that their city will lose its autonomy well before 2047, when the "one country, two systems" arrangement that guarantees Hong Kong's special administrative status will end.

Given how fraught relations between Hong Kong and mainland China have become since 1997, one might think this has always been the case. As this Element shows, however, such rhetoric – nationalistic and triumphalist on one side, localist and defiant on the other – masks the many ways Hong Kong and China not only coexisted with but benefited from each other for more than 150 years. The porous boundary between China and Hong Kong – a British colony and a Chinese border town – enabled the two to use each other economically, politically, socially, and culturally. Even after the establishment of the PRC in October 1949, the mainland relied on Hong Kong for foreign-exchange reserves and as a window to the outside world, while Hong Kong continued to depend on China for food, water, and labor. Hong Kong capital, business know-how, and connections with the capitalist world played a key role in China's reopening in the late 1970s, which in turn powered Hong Kong's transition from industry to finance and services.

The current situation aside, it is not difficult to understand why we might not think this would be a good relationship. For decades, mainland historians focused on China's "century of shame" and the destruction of its indigenous "sprouts of capitalism" by foreign imperialism. Historians of communist or socialist nations often overlook how even they developed their own varieties of capitalism and consumerism – "unending capitalism" in China (Gerth, 2020) and "red globalization" in the Soviet Union (Sanchez-Sibony, 2014), for example. Scholars of colonialism usually focus more on discord and conflict and less on collaboration and accommodation.

To be sure, as we see in each section, there were tensions and clashes. The British acquired Hong Kong, and then Kowloon in 1860, in two long and bloody wars. All three main Chinese governments during this era – the Qing, Republican, and Communist – occasionally tried to undermine Hong Kong's stability. On balance, though, this period was defined by a remarkably stable and even harmonious relationship, despite being stretched over two tumultuous centuries, despite two massive upheavals in China (the Taiping Rebellion in the mid-1800s and the civil war between the Communists and the Nationalists from 1946 to 1949), despite Britain's imperialist ambitions in Asia, and despite its waning power in the post–World War II era and China's ascendancy. The Hong Kong–China nexus, though firmly embedded in global dynamics of colonialism, Cold War politics, and capitalist expansion, defies many common assumptions about nationalism, colonialism, and decolonization.

Other nexuses and networks also mattered, of course. Most notably with Britain and its empire, especially Malaya and India, but also Australia and Canada. Despite recent efforts by local authorities to stress the Chineseness of Hong Kong, the region is as much a part of British imperial history as it is of Chinese history. Becoming a colony made Hong Kong even more connected with mainland China. It transformed a small outpost of the Qing Empire into a major trading center. As both an "instrument of British Imperial policy" and a "safe haven from the often chaotic conditions of China," Hong Kong linked Chinese people with the colonies and countries of Southeast Asia and the Pacific (Williams, 2004: 260). The colony was a bridgehead back into China for Australians of Chinese descent, who established business interests there and in Canton and other Chinese cities. Hong Kong could not have become the place it did without being a British colony – just as it could never have become the kind of colony it did without being geographically part of China.

Through the nexus with the treaty ports forced open in the 1800s and early 1900s to foreign trade and residence, Hong Kong was integrated into the corporate structure and practices of many foreign interests operating in China (often as a South China headquarters with responsibilities for operations in other provinces) and in Southeast Asia, as well as into the British legal, social, and familial networks in these regions. These foreign linkages were interwoven with those of their Chinese partners. Hong Kong also had significant connections with Japan, and later its colony of Taiwan. It was a hub for major maritime communications from the early colonial days, and one for commercial aviation after World War II.

The relationship with America was also important. Hong Kong was deeply involved in America's transpacific trade from the 1840s, the United States was the first country to open a consulate in Hong Kong, and American missionaries opened the first church, in 1843 (Tucker, 1994: 198). The California Gold Rush transformed Hong Kong from "a small-scale entrepot of goods" into "a large-scale entrepot of people" (Sinn, 2013: 90). California became a key emigration destination and, at least in the late 1800s and early 1900s, a market for high-quality opium prepared in Hong Kong. The colony was particularly useful for the United States after the Communist Revolution and during the Cold War: as a spying post, a tourist destination, and a rest-and-recreation port for military personnel. From the 1950s on, Hong Kong supplied American markets with clothing and textiles, toys, plastic flowers, and wigs, often produced in factories funded by American capital. Playing a vital role in this transformation – as well as China's dramatic economic development in the 1970s and 1980s – were American-educated Hong Kong elites, often from families with American ties stretching back before World War II and with connections to prewar Shanghai (Hamilton, 2020).

Still, the China nexus towers over them all. From the earliest years up to 1997, this British colony was inextricably linked with China. As an "in-between place" (Sinn, 2011), Hong Kong's geographical location meant it was always affected mainly by events in China, particularly in Guangdong Province. Especially before the Communist Revolution, for many Chinese residents "China" meant Guangdong (Chan, 1995: 31). And the city in China that was linked the most closely with Hong Kong was Canton, known today as Guangzhou – so interlocked that the border between Hong Kong and China was never closed, at least not until after the Communist Revolution. Far from it, for Hong Kong depended on the free flow of goods, capital, and labor from China. As the colony's chief labor officer explained in 1939, "Hong Kong must therefore be regarded as geographically and economically attached to China from which it is separated politically as a British Crown Colony" (Hong Kong Labour Department, 1939: 110). The dramatic transformation of British Hong Kong attests to both the economic fundamentals of intraregional cohesion and the power of political intervention in south China (Lu, 2014).

* * *

This nexus was sometimes a complicated one. For one, situated at the edge of two empires (Carroll, 2005), Hong Kong from the start was "a Chinese as well as a British colony" – "a city built by Chinese colonists under British sponsorship," transformed as much by Chinese from neighboring counties, and even farther in China, as by the British (Luk, 1991: 653). Chinese and foreign visitors alike noted how, as one scholar put it in the late 1970s, "Hong Kong is a Chinese city which is not within China" (Leeming, 1977: 14). Even in the late 1800s and early 1900s, the heyday of British imperialism, captions for tourist postcards usually read "Hong Kong, China." Until 1949, foreign travelers rarely went to Hong Kong without heading north to Shanghai and Beijing. After 1949, many visitors went to British Hong Kong because they could not enter Communist China.

It would be difficult to measure which side benefited more from this relationship. What is clear, however, is that whereas people in Hong Kong actively supported China in many ways from the mid-1850s on, as the Qing Empire began to suffer from what officials called "external threats and internal chaos," China's help for Hong Kong was usually more incidental than intentional. The benefits for Hong Kong often resulted from trouble across the border. In many ways, the secret to Hong Kong's success was China's failure: its failure in the late nineteenth and early twentieth centuries to provide a secure political and business environment, its failure after the 1911 Republican Revolution to control factionalism and regionalism, and its failure after 1949 to avoid the excesses and tragedies that have characterized so many communist revolutions. If Hong Kong was one of the most important places in China for more than 150 years, one reason is that it was politically not part of China (Carroll, 2005: 191).

From the mid-1800s until the end of the colonial era, Hong Kong was a haven for Chinese refugees: during the Taiping Rebellion; in the years surrounding the Republican Revolution; in the 1920s after the failure to unite China; after the outbreak of the Sino–Japanese War in 1937; during the civil war and after the Communist Revolution; during the Great Leap Forward and the Great Famine in the late 1950s and early 1960s and then the Cultural Revolution from 1966 to 1976; and after the Tiananmen Square Massacre in June 1989. (Occasionally the movement of people went the other way, even if it was only temporary.) Yet Hong Kong was also a haven in ordinary times. A safe destination for investing capital and sending children to be educated, it was especially attractive as a permanent place of work and residence to Chinese who had spent time overseas (Williams, 2004: 260, 268). Meanwhile, money made in Hong Kong could be used to help modernize China.

Influence was rarely one-directional, however. Hong Kong was the birthplace of many commercial institutions modeled on Western versions, such as department stores and modern banking and insurance, which would help transform Chinese cities. Yet this could not have happened without the labor, capital, and business connections China provided. Hong Kong was affected by the rise of Chinese nationalism from the late 1800s on and acted as "an offshore civil society" for Chinese politics (Hung and Ip, 2012: 527). During the strikes of the

1920s, which were inspired by the rise of national and labor consciousness in China, Canton became both "asylum and sanctuary" for strikers who returned "home" (Chan, 1990: 137). And the success of the strikes in Hong Kong in turn encouraged strikes across the border.

The nexus was far more than economic and political, though the economic dimension became especially significant in the third period, particularly from the late 1970s on. Hong Kong's colonial status preserved many traditional Chinese customs and practices long after they faded away or were abolished on the mainland: traditional Chinese characters (as opposed to the simplified ones used on the mainland), fengshui, concubinage, and certain land laws. Indeed, Chinese tradition in Hong Kong was "as much a British heritage as it was Chinese" (Faure, 2003: 25). Yet debates such as the ones about female servitude in the 1920s and 1930s were also about Chineseness and modernity – in Hong Kong and in China.

Both PRC and Hong Kong leaders have often used the saying "blood is thicker than water" when describing the inseparability of Hong Kong and China. One result of the Hong Kong–China nexus, however, was the rise of a local Hong Kong identity that depended on not being part of China. Scholars have rightly focused on Hong Kong's many contributions to China. But this emphasis on Hong Kong's role in China's nation-building also overlooks how colonial Hong Kong was founded and developed with Chinese help, how most Chinese in Hong Kong went there not to be part of the Chinese polity, and how by the late 1800s some Chinese in Hong Kong saw themselves as a special kind of Chinese: Hong Kong Chinese.

* * *

Periodizing history can be problematic. Dramatic political developments do not necessarily lead to radical changes in everyday life, for instance. And the standard periodization for modern Chinese history does not always work for Hong Kong: it would make little sense, say, to write "Qing Hong Kong" or "Republican Hong Kong." The 1911 revolution, which ended the Qing Dynasty after almost three centuries, was important for Hong Kong. However, it is not nearly as useful for dividing Hong Kong history as it is for Chinese history, even though, as we shall see, the 1949 revolution is.

But any history needs to be organized somehow. This Element is divided into four main sections. The first covers the period from early 1841, when the British occupied Hong Kong Island, to late 1911. Starting with the establishment of the Republic of China in 1912 and its effects on Hong Kong, the second section ends with the civil war between the Communists and the Nationalists. The third begins with the establishment of the PRC and ends with 1997, the year

Hong Kong returned to Chinese sovereignty. The final section asks why relations between postcolonial Hong Kong and post-socialist China have often been so much worse than during the colonial period.

If periodizing Hong Kong's history in accordance with mainland China's can be awkward, so can writing Chinese names consistently in English. Until recently, the city known today as Beijing was generally known in the English-speaking world as Peking. Communist leader Mao Zedong was Mao Tse-tung. Further complicating matters, most people in Hong Kong have historically spoken not Mandarin (better known these days as Putonghua) but Cantonese, which lacks a commonly used romanization system. They call Hong Kong *Heunggong* and not *Xianggang*, as it would be pronounced in Mandarin and as it is written in the Hanyu pinyin system of romanization used in China today.

Here, then, place, personal, and institution names in Hong Kong are romanized according to their conventional usage (Kowloon rather than Jiulong, Ho Kai and not He Qi, and Man Mo Temple instead of Wen Wu Temple). Names of people in mainland China, however, follow the pinyin system, except for figures such as Sun Yat-sen and Chiang Kai-shek who are better known outside China by other nonstandard romanizations. The names of treaties are listed according to contemporary standards (the Treaty of Nanking, not the Treaty of Nanjing). Except for Canton, place names in mainland China are in pinyin (Guangdong rather than Kwangtung). When appropriate, pinyin equivalents are provided in the index. Inconsistent and sometimes confusing, perhaps, but then so is history.

2 Hong Kong and Imperial China

Losing Hong Kong during the Opium War became known many years later as China's first national humiliation. It was a minor loss for the Manchu rulers of the Great Qing, however, for the tiny island barely appeared on Qing maps and had not played a major role in Chinese history until then. The Pearl River Delta has a long tradition of overseas and intra-Chinese trade, while Hong Kong had been part of China since "ancient times," as the Basic Law (Hong Kong's constitution since July 1, 1997) explains. But it was far from a strategic part. The British could have demanded much more from the Treaty of Nanking, which in August 1842 ceded the island to Britain "in perpetuity." Non-Chinese people originally from northeast Asia, the Manchus had conquered China in 1644 and made it part of a mighty empire. But they had been defeated by a small kingdom of "redheaded barbarians" with superior military technology and able to mobilize troops from their own empire in India.

There was nothing inevitable about Hong Kong becoming Britain's first and only Chinese colony. British interest in a trading base on the China coast dated almost as far back as the British presence in China, beginning in the early 1600s. But neither Hong Kong nor the idea of a formal colony was considered seriously until the early nineteenth century. Nor was Hong Kong the only place the British had eyed in the years leading up to the Opium War: one of the many other suggestions was the island of Taiwan (known to foreigners as Formosa). Some later wished the British had instead kept Zhoushan (which they called Chusan), an island off the east coast of China they had occupied during the war but then returned to Qing rule in June 1846 (Munn, 1997; D'arcy-Brown, 2012). Even after the British began to build their new colony, some wondered if it should ever have been taken at all.

Nor did losing Hong Kong fundamentally change Qing attitudes toward Britain and the other Western nations trying to prise open China. Many Qing officials assumed the British would be content with their new acquisition and not demand anything more. Despite the "first unequal treaty" rhetoric crafted by Chinese nationalists in the twentieth century, the Treaty of Nanking was not unprecedented. Following a conflict with the khanate of Kokand over trading rights in Kashgar in the western reaches of the empire, in 1835, the Qing had agreed to a series of treaties. The terms were remarkably similar to those in the Treaty of Nanking. From the perspective of the imperial court at Beijing, the differences between the two treaties were minor (Fletcher, 1978: 375–385).

Far from being "cut off," as Chinese sources sometimes put it, Hong Kong and China became more connected – and more important for each other – after Hong Kong became a British colony. The expansion of trade, especially in Indian opium, and an influx of Chinese emigrants integrated Hong Kong's economy even further with that of Guangdong and other nearby provinces. Conflicts between Britain and China over Hong Kong were relatively minor, especially given how turbulent this period was in both British imperial and Chinese history. The Second Opium War (1856–1860), which gave Britain the Kowloon peninsula in the Convention of Peking, was the last significant conflict between the two empires. The Taiping Rebellion (1850–1864), which over-lapped partly with the Second Opium War, helped revive the colony's sagging economy. The leasing of the New Territories in 1898, three years after China was defeated in the first Sino–Japanese War (1894–1895), occurred without bloodshed or harm to diplomatic relations with Britain. China provided a steady supply of labor for Hong Kong, while the colony's schools offered talent for China in the wake of the Second Opium War and the Taiping Rebellion. Hong Kong's colonial status enabled people there to contribute to the Chinese revolutionary movement, which led to the end of the Qing Dynasty and the founding of the Republic of China in January 1912.

* * *

Although Hong Kong was a remote outpost in the Qing Empire when the British arrived, it was by no means a "barren island with hardly a house upon it," as foreign secretary Lord Palmerston famously wrote in April 1841. Then part of Xin'an county, the island boasted several villages and hamlets, a substantial land and boat population, and shrines and temples – all signs of a settled community. Local government was left mainly to local headmen or village elders, with an assistant magistrate occasionally crossing the harbor from Kowloon to collect land taxes and register fishing vessels (Ng and Baker, 1983: 77; Hayes, 1984).

Most histories of colonies begin with a violent first contact between local people and foreign invaders. Hong Kong's starts rather differently. The British acquired Hong Kong during a bloody war with China. But they encountered no resistance when they formally occupied the island on January 25, 1841, in accordance with the short-lived Treaty of Chuanpi. Charles Elliot, who had led the British expedition during the Opium War and who became the first administrator of colonial Hong Kong, immediately tried to attract European and Chinese traders by promising it would be a free port where Chinese could practice their own customs and religions. The British had little trouble, moreover, finding helpers to build their colony.

The kind of accommodation and collaboration between Chinese and foreigners that would typify Hong Kong's colonial history was not new. It had been conducted for two centuries along China's southern coast, especially in the port of Canton under what foreigners called the Canton System – which from the mid-1700s limited trade with the West to Canton and depended on Chinese assistance at every level, but also throughout the Pearl River Delta and along the "watery fringes" of south China (Luk, 2022: 198). Chinese and foreigners had collaborated for even longer in Macau, which the Portuguese had leased in 1557, and in European colonies in Southeast Asia.

Several collaborators feature recurrently in the early history of colonial Hong Kong. One is Loo Aqui, who had provisioned British ships during the Opium War. Rewarded with a large plot of valuable land, Loo soon became one of Hong Kong's wealthiest and most powerful Chinese residents. Kwok Acheong, who had also supplied the British forces during the war (even serving as pilot on a British ship), became the comprador (middleman) for the Peninsular and Oriental (P & O) Steam Navigation Company and eventually a regional shipping magnate. Kwok was a frequent advisor to the colonial government and supplied the British forces during the Second Opium War. Tam Achoy, a contractor who had worked for the British in Singapore, built

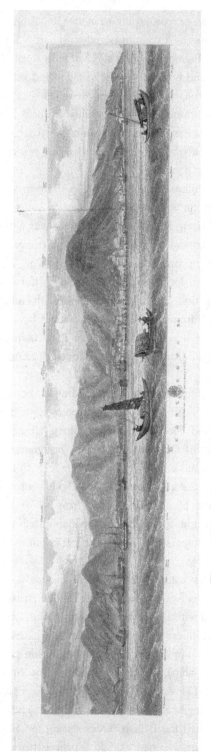

Figure 1 Hong Kong, 1846 (Library of Congress Geography and Map Division)

some of Hong Kong's most important buildings. These were all men who in Hong Kong acquired a social prominence hard to obtain in China, and compradors played an important role in Hong Kong's colonial economy (Smith, 1985; Abe, 2018). Yet, as it had for so long in south China, collaboration occurred at all levels and collaborators came from all walks of life.

There was plenty of conflict in what some colonial officials hoped would become an "Anglo-China" where East met West in mutually beneficial ways. The entrepot trade was slow to develop. Piracy and other forms of crime were endemic, though the British and Qing navies often cooperated to suppress piracy (Chappell, 2018; Kwan, 2020). Land shortages and the end of traditional land rights meant confusion over rents. The indigenous Chinese population was quickly overrun by new settlers from the mainland. The administration of justice was biased heavily against Chinese people. Discrimination by Europeans against Chinese, distrust between new and old Chinese residents, and uncertainty about Hong Kong's future only made the situation worse (Munn, 2001: 53–105).

Hong Kong also offered opportunities, however. The money to be made and the easy access from Guangdong drew merchants, laborers, artisans, prostitutes, and smugglers – despite frequent warnings and orders from Guangdong authorities not to go there. Chinese merchants, for example, soon learned to use colonialism to their benefit. British jurisdiction protected them when they were in China, enabling them to circumvent Qing regulations and restrictions. Although trade with India was dominated by British and Indian firms, Hong Kong opened Chinese merchants to other trading networks: with the Chinese treaty ports, with Southeast Asia, and with the Americas. British companies led the way in modern shipping while smaller Chinese firms dominated the local junk-boat trade, but the two evolved in parallel rather than independently (Choi, 2017). And even if Britons ran many of the largest and wealthiest firms, every level of their operations was made possible by Chinese – which meant recruiting friends and relatives from the mainland, thus building and strengthening business and personal networks between Hong Kong and China.

* * *

Hong Kong's two most lucrative trades in the early colonial years, opium and Chinese emigration, tied Hong Kong and China together more tightly than ever. It is impossible to overstate the importance of opium for Hong Kong and its relationship with China. The colony was founded because of the drug, and the center of the trade shifted there easily from the Canton region after the Opium War. Until the second part of the nineteenth century, when most of China's opium was cultivated domestically, the bulk was Indian opium reimported through Hong Kong. With a few notable exceptions (Bickers, 2020: 55), most large companies, foreign or Chinese, dealt in opium. Hong Kong's opium monopoly linked imperial trading systems with local ones, generating local Chinese capital and strengthening local Chinese elites. The drug even became the common currency for remittances from Chinese living in Hong Kong to their native places (Munn, 2000: 107).

Becoming a British colony also made Hong Kong the main center for Chinese emigration (Mei, 1979: 469). As it was for opium, Hong Kong was vital to Chinese emigration, while the two trades were crucial for Hong Kong's economic and social development. Although emigration was illegal under Qing law, it flourished – mainly to California but also to other parts of the Americas

3701 Opium Trader, Hong Kong Harbor, greatest Opium Port in the World, China.
COPYRIGHT 1901 BY H. C. WHITE CO.

Figure 2 Opium trader in Victoria Harbour, ca. 1901 (Library of Congress Prints and Photographs Division)

and to Southeast Asia. Local Chinese authorities neither could nor tried to stop the outflow of people. Emigration was good business and stimulated a range of other trades in Hong Kong and in China. And although the emigrant trade sometimes seemed little better than slavery, it relieved population pressures along the China coast as well as further inland. For many emigrants, Hong Kong was their first stop beyond China, and for those who managed to return someday, the first stop on their way home (Sinn, 2013: 301).

As with opium, merchants of all nationalities participated in the emigrant trade. But it was Chinese people from the Pearl River Delta, above all, who made it possible for emigrants to move to and from their destinations (Williams, 2004: 262). As with opium, the emigrant trade relied on an extensive network of collaborators in Hong Kong and throughout south China, and even farther up the coast, ranging from contractors and other middlemen in Hong Kong to shipowners and labor brokers, overseers and interpreters, and recruiters and crimps in mainland towns and villages. In the mid-1850s, the number of Chinese laborers passing through Hong Kong was almost as large as the colony's population. This massive movement of people helped build sizeable Chinese communities overseas. Hong Kong was not only a British colony and a "regional sub-community in South China": it was a "constituent part of a global Chinese diaspora" (Fung, 2005: 9).

* * *

Hong Kong's education system, which drew young Chinese students locally and from Guangdong, also tied Hong Kong and China more closely together. It provided human resources for the Chinese Civil Service, the Imperial Chinese Maritime Customs, and the new government schools established during the Self-Strengthening Movement after China's defeat in the Second Opium War (Fok, 1990: 13–35). The Central School for Boys, founded in 1862 and later renamed Queen's College, quickly became popular with the Chinese middle classes in Hong Kong and Guangdong, who preferred it to traditional Chinese schools and considered it an avenue to a good job with foreign firms or with the Maritime Customs. So many Central School graduates went to China that people in Hong Kong sometimes complained that it was training students for China rather than for Hong Kong (Ng Lun, 1984: 81). The school's most famous graduate, Sun Yat-sen, is known as the father of modern China. The Central School for Girls, founded in 1890 and soon renamed the Belilios Public School for Girls after its benefactor, an Italian Jewish merchant born in India, also attracted students from Hong Kong and Guangdong. Early graduates Chau Lee Sun and Wong Yuen Hing became two of the first female Chinese doctors of Western medicine after studying at a missionary-run medical college in Canton.

Many other graduates from Hong Kong schools went on to work for the Chinese government. Born in Malaya, Ng Choy attended a missionary school in Canton as a youngster and then St. Paul's College in Hong Kong. After studying law in England, in 1877 he became the first Chinese to be called to the English bar. Declining invitations to help draft a new commercial code for the Qing government, Ng instead returned to Hong Kong to practice law. In 1880, he became the first Chinese appointed to the Legislative Council. The appointment was temporary, but it reflected the growing influence of Hong Kong's Chinese community. Seriously in debt after a financial crash in 1882, Ng moved to China, where, known as Wu Tingfang (Wu being the Mandarin pronunciation of Ng), he became a legal advisor to the Qing government. In 1896, he was appointed minister to the United States, where he strove to debunk the image of China as "the sick man of the East." He held a variety of posts in the Qing government and then in the new republican government after the 1911 revolution (Pomerantz-Zhang, 1992).

* * *

Early voluntary institutions also linked Hong Kong and China, at the same time shaping a local Chinese elite. The Man Mo Temple, founded in 1847 by Loo Aqui and Tam Achoy to worship the civil (Man) god and the martial (Mo) god, soon became the main religious and social center for the Chinese community. The temple also became prominent in the 1850s as an "unrecognised and unofficial" local government board that "secretly controlled native affairs and acted as commercial arbitrators" (Ting, 1990: 152). The Nam Pak Hong Kung So (North–South Trading Companies Association) was formed in 1868 as a mutual-assistance association for the various import–export firms operating between China and Southeast Asia. It became the largest commercial and occupational association in Hong Kong. As it expanded, so did its services: managing guild activities, providing banking and insurance services, and running a fire brigade and a neighborhood watch force. It also forged relations with similar associations in China and across Southeast Asia (Fok, 1990: 102–103; Tsai, 1993: 62).

The largest and most important voluntary association was the Tung Wah Hospital, founded in 1869 to provide Chinese medicine for Hong Kong's Chinese population. It soon provided a range of services: caring for the destitute, sending corpses and remains to China for proper burials, and repatriating women and laborers kidnapped from China. The hospital replaced the Man Mo Temple as the main social and cultural center of the Chinese community, and its committee functioned even more so as an informal government, settling civil disputes and managing the Chinese community, especially as migration from

Guangdong increased (Lethbridge, 1971: 144–158; Sinn, 1989: 82–120). Yet this depended on connections with China and happenings there. Although the Qing government often viewed Chinese overseas and in Hong Kong negatively, it realized they could be useful. Especially from the 1850s on, it became more willing to sell official degrees and titles to finance campaigns for suppressing uprisings and rebellions and for flood and famine relief. Chinese merchants in Hong Kong were situated perfectly to provide these services, which they could not have done without the opportunities these calamities in China provided.

* * *

The Taiping Rebellion that ravaged China for almost fifteen years had little negative effect on Hong Kong. Naturally, there was some anxiety, and it is ironic that within a few years the British were fighting the Qing in the Second Opium War (started by a Hong Kong governor, John Bowring) yet also helping them suppress the rebellion. But there was little concern in Hong Kong until the southern capital at Nanjing fell to the rebels in 1853. In autumn 1854, Taiping rebels struggled with Qing forces for control of Kowloon, just across the harbor (and not yet part of British Hong Kong). Taiping troops occasionally even marched through the streets of Hong Kong.

Amid this uncertain atmosphere could still be found the cultural interchange that characterized colonial Hong Kong. Although the British did not try to make Hong Kong Christian, it was an important center for missionaries, many of whom first studied Chinese there, and for the missionary movement in China. There, Hong Rengan, a distant cousin of the Taiping Heavenly King, Hong Xiuquan, became acquainted with several missionaries. One was James Legge, a Scotsman with the London Missionary Society who was more interested in sinology than in evangelism. Hong formed a deep friendship with Legge and helped him translate the Confucian classics. Like Sun Yat-sen and others later in this century, it was in Hong Kong where Hong learned about Western science, medicine, history, and politics. Impressed by the orderliness of the colony, he decided that China had much to learn from the outside world (Girardot, 2002: 49–61; Platt, 2012: 19–24).

Several years after Hong Rengan left Hong Kong in 1858 to help his cousin run the Taiping Heavenly Kingdom from Nanjing, came a pioneering scholar named Wang Tao, also with Taiping connections. While working for the London Missionary Society in Shanghai, Wang had been in contact with the Taiping leaders whose troops were threatening the city. In 1862, he was charged with treason. Under a pseudonym, he had written a letter proposing how the rebels might defeat the Qing, insisting that they, not the Westerners, were the real enemies of China. With help from the foreign forces in Shanghai, the Qing were able to fend off the rebels – and to find Wang's seditious letter. After taking refuge for more than four months in the British consulate, he finally managed to escape on a British steamer to Hong Kong, where he assisted Legge in his translations, wrote prolifically about the West, and helped launch modern Chinese journalism. He finally returned to Shanghai in 1884, having spent almost two decades introducing Western ideas to Chinese readers and Confucianism to Western readers, and using Hong Kong's freedom of the press to advocate for reform (Cohen, 1987; Sinn, 1998).

Although the Taiping Rebellion cost more than 20 million lives, disrupted trade, and destroyed cities and parts of the Chinese countryside, it brought new human and physical capital to Hong Kong. From 1853 to 1859, the Chinese population rose from forty thousand to eighty-five thousand, even though some twenty-five thousand people left in protest during the Second Opium War. The tumult caused by the rebellion brought new traders and their families to Hong Kong, aiding the formation of a new Chinese business elite. Li Sing, originally from Xinhui county, threw himself into money changing, insurance, real estate, emigration, and the opium monopoly. With his cousin Li Leong, who had been in Hong Kong since the early 1840s, Li Sing founded what became one of the largest emigrant brokerage and shipping companies (and collaborated with the British during the Second Opium War).

This influx rejuvenated what had become a struggling colony, hardly the "great emporium of the East." Although the Treaty of Nanking had given the British a base in China, it also opened four more ports (in addition to Canton), diverting trade from Hong Kong to the treaty ports. And even the opening of more treaty ports had not expanded trade as much as the British had hoped. Qing officials tried to discourage wealthy Chinese merchants from going to Hong Kong, sometimes threatening to punish or even execute their families. Visitors from China and overseas alike now noted the changes that had taken place since the 1850s, praising the increased wealth and improved appearance of the colony. Wang Tao marveled at how these developments were "all the result of fate and chance" (in White, 1996: 64).

* * *

The controversy in the late 1870s and early 1880s over the *mui-tsai* (lit. "little sister") system of female bond servitude reveals Hong Kong's growing connections with China following the Taiping Rebellion. *Mui-tsai* were girls and women, usually from poor families, sold to wealthier ones to provide domestic help. Although the system existed throughout China under a variety of names, it was especially prevalent in the south with the economic and social disruption caused by the Taiping Rebellion and other conflicts (Lethbridge, 1978: 74–75).

Hong Kong's first ordinance, passed in 1844, banned slavery. But few people, Chinese or foreign, thought this applied to the *mui-tsai*. While some critics argued that the system encouraged sexual abuse, defenders insisted the girls were treated as family members and were saved from prostitution. The ambiguous status of the *mui-tsai* within the adoptive household (half servant, half family member) only complicated matters. For colonials such as E. J. Eitel, a missionary and sinologist who also worked for the Hong Kong government, the *mui-tsai* system was grounded in ancient, ingrained forms of Chinese "patriarchicalism" that would gradually dissolve as China modernized (Eitel, 1895: 546–548).

Despite occasional criticism, the legal status of the system was not seriously questioned until the late 1870s. A formerly transient and overwhelmingly male society had become more settled, thanks to the influx of wealthier families during the Taiping Rebellion. As more Chinese families came to Hong Kong, the *mui-tsai* system expanded. An extensive network of kidnapping developed to feed the need for servants and prostitutes: girls and young women were often seized from their home villages in Guangdong and then sold in Hong Kong. The system even drew attention from reformist groups in Britain. Politicians in California used evidence of its thriving in a British colony to support restricting Chinese immigration to America.

The *mui-tsai* controversy arose from different attitudes toward Hong Kong's geographic, political, and cultural position at the edge of the British and the Chinese empires (Carroll, 2009: 1465). In late 1878, four prominent Chinese merchants petitioned Governor John Hennessy for permission to form an organization to stop the kidnapping of children from Dongguan, the merchants' home district. When Chief Justice John Smale led a campaign in October 1879 to stamp out what he called "domestic slavery," the merchants argued that the system should be allowed to continue as a legitimate Chinese custom. They warned that banning the *mui-tsai* system would encourage another Chinese custom – drowning unwanted female babies at birth. Hennessy approved their request to form an association to protect kidnapped women and children: the Po Leung Kuk.

Compared to the heated and prolonged debates about the *mui-tsai* system after World War I, this one was short-lived and confined mainly within Hong Kong. Nor did it have much effect. Despite the Po Leung Kuk's many charitable and philanthropic activities, it upheld a "peculiarly Chinese form of patriarchy" (Sinn, 1994: 143). Some critics even considered it little more than a scheme to ensure that wealthy families had a steady supply of young servants and wealthy men had a pool of potential concubines. Still, the controversy shows how by this time Hong Kong had a powerful local Chinese elite determined – and able – to protect a practice in which they participated actively and from which they benefited, even while in Hong Kong they lived beyond the reach of Chinese sovereignty.

* * *

Connections with China brought vital labor, capital, and other resources to Hong Kong. This explains why the colonial government was determined to keep the border open, and why it was so reluctant to alienate its Chinese subjects by tampering with local practices such as the *mui-tsai*. The same connections could also spread disease. During the third plague pandemic, believed to have originated in the 1850s in the southwest province of Yunnan, expanding trade networks and increased water transport brought the plague from Canton to Hong Kong in 1894. Some one hundred thousand people had already died in Canton, and Hong Kong suffered around twenty-five hundred fatalities, almost all of them Chinese.

The story of the 1894 plague is usually told as one of conflict between Chinese and Western notions of disease and medicine, the intrusiveness of colonial public health measures, and Western fears of the Chinese lower classes. Many Chinese people resented and resisted the government's anti-plague measures, including house-to-house searches, quarantining victims on board a hospital ship supervised by Western doctors, and burning down Chinese houses to prevent the plague from spreading. From May, when the plague first broke out, to September, when the government declared that the colony was no longer an infected port, around eighty thousand Chinese people fled to Canton (Benedict, 1996b). Some foreigners believed Chinese people were even more afraid of Western doctors than of the plague.

This story is also one of connectivity and mobility (Peckham 2016: 74–89). By the early 1850s, Yunnan and Canton had become increasingly linked through the opium trade and through migration from Guangdong to the southwestern frontier. The disruption caused by the Taiping Rebellion likewise encouraged the spread of the plague (Benedict, 1996a: 49–99). Just as better commercial links between Yunnan and Guangdong took the plague to Canton, they carried it from Canton to Hong Kong: more than ten thousand passengers traveled up and down the Pearl River each week between the two cities. Information (and misinformation) also spread easily between Hong Kong and Canton, not only because of better transport and communications but also because of the close economic and familial ties between the two regions. Placards in Canton warned people against going to Hong Kong, where Western doctors were said to conduct heinous acts such as cutting open pregnant women and gouging out their babies' eyes to make medicine.

And this connectivity and mobility did not stop at Hong Kong: from there the plague traveled to India, where it may have killed up to 11 million people.

*   *   *

The acquisition of the New Territories in June 1898 for ninety-nine years under the second Convention of Peking added more than eighty thousand people and some 365 square miles to British Hong Kong. The goal was a buffer area, not so much against China but to protect Hong Kong from the other powers challenging Britain's supremacy in the region: Russia, Germany, France, and Japan. The Sino–Japanese War had led to a scramble for concessions, with Western nations and Japan trying to obtain as much influence in China as possible.

Unlike the first two treaties, this one did not involve any conflict between China and Britain. But the actual occupation of the New Territories provoked widespread resistance from villagers on both sides of the border. During the "Six Day War" of April 1899, British troops armed with little more than rifles and bayonets killed several hundred members of a ragtag force of villagers armed with antiquated weapons. Partly the result of miscommunication between the governor, the colonial secretary, and the British military commander on the ground, the brutal suppression was covered up for more than a century. The colonial government did not want to ruin the image of a peaceful administration, while the village elders quickly decided the insurrection had been a bad idea. The only military campaign in Hong Kong's history until the Japanese invasion in December 1941 thus disappeared from official and public memory (Hase, 2008).

Most of the New Territories ended up being administered differently from the rest of Hong Kong. There the British applied their form of "indirect rule," similar to that in other parts of the empire, especially in West Africa and Malaya. The plan was to run the region as Chinese officials had for centuries – by relying mainly on village elders and local headmen. For many if not most villagers, it probably mattered little that they were ruled by foreigners, and working with the British bolstered the power of village elders (Watson, 1983: 481). One result was that many Chinese customs that had begun to disappear in urban Hong Kong and in mainland China lasted well into the 1970s, including the practice preventing women from inheriting land, which remained legal until the 1990s. No wonder Alexander Grantham, governor from 1947 to 1957, described the New Territories as "almost more Chinese than China" (Grantham, 1965: 11).

The New Territories became part of British Hong Kong. But this led to even greater integration with China, at least until the Communist Revolution of 1949 and the closing of the border in 1950. The opening of the Kowloon–Canton Railway connected Hong Kong and Canton more closely than ever, and then with the rest of China through the Canton–Hankow line completed in 1936. The line between Kowloon and Canton opened in October 1911, only one week before the mutiny that precipitated the Republican Revolution, and the track and bridges were occasionally destroyed during the strife of the 1920s discussed in the following Section. Still, the new railway gave Hong Kong better access to even more Chinese and international markets, and helped local industrialists move raw materials and manufactured goods (Miners, 2006).

At least technically, however, this Convention of Peking was "an appointment with China" (Tsang, 1997a: 12). Because the lease was for ninety-nine years, British jurisdiction would expire on June 30, 1997. Although many British officials assumed the lease would be permanent, some eighty years later the British would have to negotiate. In 1984, they agreed to return the entire colony to the PRC. Thus the leasing, rather than outright cession, of the New Territories helped smooth the way for reunification in 1997.

* * *

Although the leasing of the New Territories did not involve any conflict between Hong Kong and the Qing government, it occurred during a time of growing Chinese nationalism. Hong Kong played an active role in this from the late 1800s on, as it did in the 1884 anti-French strike, the colony's first big political movement. By the early 1880s, French and Qing troops were skirmishing along the border between China and Vietnam, which in 1874, France had forced to sign a treaty granting it sovereignty. When French forces attacked the coastal city of Fuzhou and the island of Taiwan in August 1884, workers in Hong Kong went on strike and refused to service French ships. Local Chinese merchants petitioned the colonial government not to let French naval vessels use Victoria Harbour. When the government ignored the petition, fined workers who refused to work for the French, and prosecuted newspaper editors for publishing anti-French proclamations by Qing authorities, the strikers targeted the French forces and the Hong Kong government.

The 1884 strike also reveals the complexity of Hong Kong's relationship with China, in particular the different attitudes there toward the colony. Officials in Beijing were eager to keep the situation in Hong Kong from getting out of control. Because they depended on loans from Hong Kong banks to finance the war and relied on weapons and munitions imported through the colony, they dared not risk Britain and France joining forces again as they had during the Second Opium War. But authorities in Guangdong, where anti-British sentiments persisted well after the war, had a different view (Chan, 1995: 32–34).

They issued proclamations forbidding Chinese in Hong Kong from working for the French and offered rewards for killing French troops, threatened to execute "traitors" and punish their families and relatives, and tried to enlist secret societies by offering them rewards (Tsai, 1993: 124–146).

Hong Kong people also participated actively in the nationalist boycotts of the early 1900s. Sparked by the suicide (in front of the American consulate in Shanghai) of a young Chinese man who had been arrested without a warrant by immigration officers in Boston, the Anti-American Boycott of 1905–1906 was a massive rejection of American goods in response to the exclusion acts of the 1880s and early 1890s, which prohibited Chinese workers from entering the United States. Many shops refused to stock American goods, while newspapers rejected advertisements, listed merchants who continued to sell them, and publicized the progress of the boycott. Some local Chinese business leaders opposed the boycott, worried that it would hurt Hong Kong's economy. Others like Li Yuk-tong, who had started his career in California and then founded some of the first Chinese insurance companies in Hong Kong, formed a society to oppose the exclusion acts (Tsai, 1993: 182–206).

Such boycotts were part of China-wide campaigns, but they had distinctive local dimensions. The next one, the Anti-Japanese Boycott, lasted from March to December 1908. It began after the Japanese government forced the Qing to apologize for seizing a Japanese freighter that had been smuggling arms and munitions into Guangdong. Even if many Chinese were critical of the Qing government, they protested this "national humiliation" by boycotting Japanese goods. The Hong Kong campaign was even more intense than the one in Guangdong. Merchants who violated the boycott were threatened with fines (the newly established Dare to Die Society threatened to kill them and slice off their ears), and rioters attacked several shops selling Japanese goods (Tsai, 1993: 207–237).

As it had been for Hong Rengan and Wang Tao during the Taiping Rebellion, Hong Kong was a source of inspiration in later decades for Chinese reformers and revolutionaries – most notably Sun Yat-sen, who helped overthrow the Qing Dynasty in 1911, but also for more moderate reformers such as Kang Youwei and Liang Qichao, who believed that China should become a constitutional monarchy (Fok, 1990: 66–96). Sun, who was educated partly in Hong Kong, first at the Central School and then at the College of Medicine for Chinese, later claimed he had formed his revolutionary ideas "entirely" in Hong Kong, having been impressed by the peace and order in the colony. Keen not to stoke revolutionary or anti-Manchu feelings that might provoke anti-British sentiments, the colonial government kept recent Chinese history out of local schools. Still, topics such as parliamentary

Figure 3 Sun Yat-sen (center) and fellow revolutionaries (Library of Congress Prints and Photographs Division)

government encouraged students such as Sun to think more about politics and about the fate of China.

Sun was greatly influenced by one of the teachers at the College of Medicine, Ho Kai, a Hong Kong–born physician, lawyer, and businessman who identified closely with his birthplace and was proud of its achievements. Except for ten years' study in Britain, Ho spent his whole life in Hong Kong. His Chinese nationalism was inseparable from the colony where he was born and educated. Whereas Sun advocated overthrowing the Manchus and establishing a republic, Ho believed China should become a constitutional monarchy like Britain. With help from his friend and fellow reformer Hu Liyuan, in 1900, he laid out his beliefs in a six-volume work titled *The True Meaning of Government*. It was futile, they explained, for China to borrow Western military technology to learn the secrets of Western power, as some Qing reformers had urged. Instead, they argued that China's very essence needed to be changed: it needed capitalism, parliamentary rule, and popular rights (Chan Lau, 1990: 23–32; Tsai, 1993: 154–163; Carroll, 2005: 108–130).

Men like Ho Kai were part of a network of professionals and reformers in Hong Kong and the Chinese treaty ports. By the late 1800s, Hong Kong had become the center of a Chinese capitalist expansion ranging from mainland China to Southeast Asia, Australia, and the Americas. Some of these local business elites were originally from Hong Kong or had moved there at a young age. Others were originally from Guangdong, having spent time in California, such as Li Yuk-tong, or in Australia, such as Ma Ying Piu, founder of the first Chinese department store, the Sincere Company, and the Kwok brothers, founders of the Wing On Department Store. These businessmen protected their interests through organizations such as the Chinese Chamber of Commerce (1896), which in turn helped build new links with similar organizations in China and in Southeast Asia.

Hong Kong also served as a sanctuary for Chinese reformers and revolutionaries of various stripes, including Sun Yat-sen, Yang Qurun (killed by Qing assassins in January 1901), Chen Shaobai, and Kang Youwei. Governor William Robinson's infamous order in March 1896 that Sun be banished from Hong Kong for five years sometimes obscures how Chinese revolutionaries and reformists (and dissidents in general) could do more or less what they wanted in Hong Kong, as long as they did not break any laws or threaten British interests. In the same year, the colonial government rejected a request by the Qing government to extradite one of Sun's associates. When Kang Youwei escaped to Hong Kong in 1898, the colonial authorities not only tolerated his presence but also allowed him to stay temporarily in police barracks. Though Kang too was eventually banished, his friends and associates in Shanghai were so grateful to the Hong Kong government that they published a letter of thanks in the *North China Daily News* (Chan Lau, 1990: 39).

Hong Kong did more than inspire and shelter: it became a propaganda center and a base for staging uprisings across the border. Thanks to the colony's relatively wide freedom of press, newspapers such as the *China Daily* could openly call for revolution – an act punishable by death in China. Aimed not so much at readers in Hong Kong but in China and in overseas Chinese communities, the *China Daily* was only one such newspaper funded by supporters within Hong Kong. Kang Youwei and Liang Qichao had their own reformist newspaper. Sun was able to open local branches of the Revive China Society (Xingzhonghui) and the United League (Tongmenghui). The first (unsuccessful) revolutionary uprising, in Canton in 1895, was coordinated from Hong Kong, as was the second (also unsuccessful), in Huizhou in 1900. From 1895 to 1911, at least eight rebellions were planned from Hong Kong (Tsai, 1993: 238). Some revolutionaries even received their military training there.

These revolutionary publications were all short-lived, their influence limited. The activities of the Hong Kong branch of the United League were neither as extensive nor as effective as they are often described in revolutionary accounts, while the Revive China Association lost much of its vigor after the failed uprisings of 1895 and 1900 (Chan Lau, 1990: 4). This does not diminish the importance of Hong Kong in the Chinese revolutionary movement, however. In all these activities, Hong Kong's international financial connections helped, and Sun and his associates used them to receive funds from overseas Chinese communities.

* * *

Hong Kong support for the reformist and anti-Qing activities of the late 1800s continued through the revolution, which began on October 10, 1911, when units of the Qing government's New Army led a mutiny in the city of Wuchang (today's Wuhan). The revolution inspired people from all walks of life. Crowds marched on the local branches of the Bank of China and a pro-monarchy newspaper, forcing them to pull down the Qing imperial flag and replace it with the new one. Ma Ying Piu, Li Yuk-tong, and other businessmen formed a local Red Cross branch to send medicine and personnel across the border, while the Tung Wah Hospital and other organizations provided food, medicine, and clothing for China displaced by the revolution. Local support for the revolution grew even stronger when Guangdong province declared its independence on November 9 (Tsai, 1993: 250–251).

The establishment of the Republic of China on January 1, 1912, with the capital at Nanjing and Sun Yat-sen provisional president, was celebrated across Hong Kong. Governor Frederick Lugard wrote that the feeling in Hong Kong was "ardently Republican" (in Fok, 1990: 63). As the next Section shows, however, the failure of the revolution to unite China caused many people to identify more closely with colonial Hong Kong. Many of the Chinese in Hong Kong who were so influential in the revolutionary movement saw themselves as special Chinese, different from their counterparts on the mainland. In December 1911, only two months after the revolution, eighteen local Chinese leaders, some of whom had also supported the revolutionary movement, petitioned Lugard for a large plot of land to be used for a cemetery for "Chinese permanently residing in Hongkong." They had made the colony their "home" and had "no intention of returning to China save for temporary purposes – social, commercial or otherwise." In July 1912, Lugard's successor, Henry May, endorsed the request: "It would tend to create a colonial feeling and to specialize a class who desire to identify themselves with the Colony" (in Carroll, 2005: 113–114).

3 Hong Kong and Republican China

The 1911 revolution and the founding of the Republic of China ushered in a new era that lasted until the establishment of the PRC in October 1949. But the first years were far from promising. Yuan Shikai, the army commander who replaced

Sun Yat-sen as president in March 1912, failed to keep the republic together. In 1913, he had his chief political rival assassinated and suppressed a second revolution led by Sun in five breakaway provinces. In May 1915, he acquiesced to Japan's thirteen (originally twenty-one) demands for concessions in Shandong province along the lines of those granted to other foreign powers. After abolishing the newly formed national assemblies, in December 1915, Yuan declared himself emperor of the Chinese Empire. He reigned for just over eighty days and died in June 1916. Without anyone in Beijing strong enough to hold the nation together, China entered the age of the warlords – regional military leaders who became the new powerbrokers.

Although the revolution had much less significance for colonial Hong Kong, it mattered in several important ways. Eager to prevent the foreign powers from taking advantage of China's fragile state, the revolutionaries had tried to discourage anti-foreign sentiments. Likewise, local Chinese elites in Hong Kong who had supported the revolution were determined not to let it jeopardize the colony's stability. Not surprisingly, though, the excitement from seeing the Manchus out of power also fueled anti-British feelings. The social unrest that ensued, albeit short-lived, was intense. Crowds sometimes threw stones at the police and even at Governor Lugard when he appeared in public, looted shops, and tried to break prisoners out of jail. In 1913, Governor May tried to prevent private schools from becoming breeding sites for anti-British propaganda by requiring them to register with the government. The following year, his government introduced a bill banning publications that might threaten the stability of Hong Kong or China. The failure to unify China also changed Hong Kong's political relations with China. With the central government in Beijing ruling only nominally, the colonial government had to deal directly with a series of unstable and often hostile regimes in Canton. Although the situation improved by the late 1920s, it sometimes created friction between the Hong Kong government and the British Foreign Office, which recognized whoever was in charge of Beijing as the legitimate government of China.

Beginning only four months after the establishment of the new republic, the Tram Boycott of 1912–1913 shows how developments in the new China could rattle the colony. The economies of Hong Kong and Guangdong had been entwined since the early colonial days, with Chinese currency used freely. With conditions worsening after the revolution, the Chinese coins quickly depreciated in value. When May's government banned their use in April, many people took it as an insult to the young republic. When May urged the Star Ferry connecting Hong Kong Island with Kowloon and the colony's two tram companies not to accept Chinese coins, this led to even more resentment.

The shortage of Hong Kong coinage relative to Chinese coinage left passengers with less cash for their ferry and tram fares. A colony-wide boycott broke out and did not end until February 1913, and only with help from leaders of the Chinese community. Legislative Council members Ho Kai and Wei Yuk warned their fellow Hong Kong residents that the boycott would harm the economies of both Hong Kong and Canton, and that a weakened local economy would make it harder to support their kin across the border (Chan Lau 1990: 111–114; Tsai 1993: 270–287).

The tram boycott is only one example of how Hong Kong was affected by events on the mainland, especially in Guangdong. The strife there in the decades after the revolution helped boost Hong Kong's population from 600,000 in 1921 to 850,000 in 1931. In the 1920s, this figure rose at about 21,500 per year, mainly due to immigration from China (Leeming, 1977: 3). Crime, exacerbated by the political chaos in Guangdong, often overflowed into Hong Kong. In the early to mid-1920s, piracy occurred almost weekly in Hong Kong waters. Sun Yat-sen's failure to make China a stable republic cost him the support of many Hong Kong people, especially the business elites, and of the colonial government; both welcomed Yuan Shikai's suppression of Sun's second revolution. This helped forge a sense of local Hong Kong identity, especially among wealthier Chinese, who contrasted the stability in Hong Kong with the chaos in China.

Developments on each side of the border shaped the other. As they had in 1908, many Hong Kong people boycotted Japanese goods in 1915 and then in 1919, during the May Fourth Movement, which began as a protest against the Treaty of Versailles that gave Germany's concessions in Shandong to Japan. They also participated in the various national products movements of the 1920s and 1930s (Gerth, 2003: 158–200). Like many overseas Chinese, Hong Kong-educated Chinese worked throughout the mainland as teachers, doctors, scientists, and engineers. Local entrepreneurs invested in commercial and industrial concerns and donated to medical, educational, and public works in their native districts. Business, familial, and personal connections between Hong Kong and China thickened with better transportation, first with the Kowloon–Canton Railway and then with air flights in the 1930s.

Labor consciousness in Hong Kong soared, buoyed by the rise of Chinese nationalism and by workers' movements in China and across the globe. Notably, some of the concessions that workers in Hong Kong won through the strikes of the early and mid-1920s led to similar gains across the border. Many of the offerings in public works, housing, social legislation, and welfare in Hong Kong were influenced by developments in Britain and across the empire, but also by the colonial government's determination to limit the spread of labor consciousness and nationalism from China (Faure, 2003: 31). Although there were never any serious anticolonial movements, Hong Kong and Canton both became hotbeds for Chinese communism. As it had in early decades, Hong Kong served as a sanctuary for Chinese refugees in the years before World War II and during the civil war that followed.

* * *

This period saw important economic developments, owing greatly to the influx of Chinese entrepreneurs and the rise of local Chinese industry – partly because of World War I. The war itself did not have much impact on Hong Kong or China. Both foreign and Chinese residents in Hong Kong contributed funds to the British war effort, and many Chinese workers served in the Chinese Labour Corps in France. Up to one hundred thousand Chinese residents took temporary refuge in Guangdong, fearing that the colony might be attacked. There were no long-term negative economic effects. On the contrary, as it did in China, the war enabled Chinese businessmen to expand their operations because so many foreign men left to fight in Europe.

Chinese entrepreneurs thus played a growing role in Hong Kong's modern economy, even competing with foreign industries and exporting goods beyond China and Southeast Asia. Although the colony's heavy industries were mainly owned and managed by Europeans, most newer and lighter industries were run by Chinese (Leeming, 1975). This growth benefited from Hong Kong's colonial situation, in particular its British and Chinese banks and its connections with other European colonies. Hong Kong's stability, and the fact that its economy was dominated by foreign capital, was a powerful incentive for wealthy Chinese in Guangdong to invest there (Kwan, 1997: 59–60). This growth also depended heavily on developments in China, however, including the expansion of native and foreign industries there, and on the continued flow of cheap labor. Its many local features notwithstanding, this was part of "the golden age of the Chinese bourgeoisie" (Bergére, 1989). It occurred despite the lack of active encouragement or assistance from the colonial government, which remained determined to keep Hong Kong as a trading center (Ngo, 1999). Likewise, the growth and expansion of traditional Chinese banks depended on connections with China, as would the earliest modern Chinese banks in Hong Kong, starting with the Bank of East Asia (1919), the first public Chinese-capitalized bank to trade on the Hong Kong Stock Exchange (Sinn, 1994).

Without a strong central government in China, some Chinese businessmen in Hong Kong tried to influence politics in Guangdong and to protect their business interests on the mainland. In 1912, Li Yuk-tong angered Governor May by trying to form a firm in Hong Kong to help finance the new Canton government (Chung, 1998: 61). They were especially worried during the early 1920s, when Sun Yat-sen and his protégé Chiang Kai-shek's Nationalist Party (Kuomintang) was receiving help from Soviet advisors. In 1921, for example, as China continued to descend into factionalism, businessman and legislative councilor Lau Chu Pak upset the Hong Kong government by raising funds among local Chinese merchants to support General Chen Jiongming, hoping that Chen would sever his ties to Sun Yat-sen's revolutionary regime in Canton and instead deal directly with the government in Beijing (Miners, 1987: 129).

* * *

As it had for many decades, Hong Kong continued to serve as a sanctuary for people from Guangdong and other parts of China. During the strikes of the 1920s, however, the opposite was also true: Canton became a haven for striking Hong Kong workers, while support from Guangdong increased the strikers' bargaining power and prevented the British from quashing the strikes. Although World War I had helped Chinese entrepreneurs and industrialists, it had hurt workers. The Hong Kong dollar had depreciated by 50 percent since the war broke out and prices had risen significantly, yet workers' wages were no higher than before the war.

The Mechanics Strike of 1920, organized by the recently formed Chinese Mechanics Institute, began in March and lasted for almost three weeks. Some ten thousand workers went on strike for better wages. Most went to Canton, where they were supported by Sun's government and by labor unions. The mechanics won their main demand, a pay increase. Although the strike led the colonial government to ban many local unions, it inspired workers in Canton, who then held their own strike. In 1921, successful strikes occurred in every main industry in Canton, which in turn gave workers there more power to support the next two strikes in Hong Kong (Chan, 1990: 137–138).

The 1920 strike began a pattern of support from Canton for strikes in Hong Kong. During the first month of the Seamen's Strike of 1922, which lasted from January to March, local trade unions encouraged all workers to leave for Canton. More than one hundred thousand workers did just that. In Canton, the strikers were welcomed by Sun Ke, mayor of the city and son of Sun Yat-sen. Supported by the city's labor unions, Sun Ke's government fed the Hong Kong strikers and offered them housing in schools, temples, and public buildings (Chan, 1990: 138–140; Chan Lau, 1990: 169–176).

While the 1920 and 1922 strikes were orchestrated within Hong Kong and driven primarily by economic concerns, the 1925–1926 general strike shows how the revolutionary and anti-imperialist movements in China could affect the colony. The strike was partly a reaction to foreign privilege in Hong Kong. But

Figure 4 Strikers, Canton, 1925 (courtesy of Tim Ko)

the immediate causes were the May Thirtieth Incident of 1925 in Shanghai's International Settlement, where Indian policemen under British command shot dead a dozen Chinese protesters following the death of a worker at a Japanese-owned cotton mill. Even more significant, and closer to home, was a massacre in Shaji, Canton, on June 23, when troops under foreign control killed more than fifty Chinese protesters and wounded at least one hundred more. Although most people in Hong Kong were not interested in the ideology behind the nationalist revolution, the killings in Shaji shook them into supporting their compatriots (Kwan, 1997: 99). In the first two weeks after the massacre, more than fifty thousand people left Hong Kong in protest, with offers of free passage by train or steamer from the strike leaders in Canton. By the end of July, more than two hundred and fifty thousand had departed for Canton. As in 1920 and 1922, they were welcomed there by unions and the government (Chan Lau, 1990: 176–184).

In Hong Kong, government officials and Chinese community leaders blamed the strike on "Bolshevik" agitators. Many Chinese merchants opposed the strike and privately supported the efforts to end it, though they had to be cautious since they had familial and business ties with Guangdong (Gillingham, 1983: 44). Both the Nationalists and the Communists played an important role, and not just by bankrolling the strike and encouraging anti-imperialist nationalism on both sides of the border. The Nationalists even provided weapons (though the strikers seem not to have used them), while the Communists helped coordinate the strike at almost every level. And although the strike-boycott showed the failure of the Communists to promote communism in the local populace, they continued to use Hong Kong as a base for uprisings in China and even planned uprisings within Hong Kong (though none occurred). The strike also propelled some local activists into the heart of the Chinese Communist Party nationally. One was Luo Dengxian, a dockyard mechanic who later became a high-level party member (Bickers, 2020: 243).

Just as events in China had precipitated the 1925–1926 strike, so they would help end it. Despite various efforts by the colonial government and the leaders of the local Chinese business community – including threats of military force against the Canton government by Governor Reginald Stubbs (all rejected by the Colonial Office in London) and several attempts at negotiations by his successor, Cecil Clementi – it was the Nationalist government in Canton that ended the strike in October 1926. This followed Chiang Kai-shek's rise to power by ousting his rivals, and when he became comfortable enough to rely less on the Communists in a short-lived united front with his Nationalists. Hong Kong's relations with Canton improved significantly in 1927, after Chiang purged the Communists from the Nationalists. Acting on tips from

Guangdong authorities, the Hong Kong government now actively suppressed unionist and communist activities, arresting Communists and deporting them to Guangdong, where they were executed. British Hong Kong thus "played a substantial role in Chinese Communist martyrdom in Guangdong" (Chan Lau, 1999: 6).

The termination of the strike concluded several years of uncertainty between the governments in Hong Kong and Canton. The situation improved even more in the 1930s, when a series of provincial leaders trained in the West and Japan tried to reform Guangdong and make it a model province for China's modernization (Fung, 2005: 99). The strikes also showed how Chinese nationalism could provoke enough of a crisis in colonial Hong Kong to influence British policy toward China. The Foreign Office in 1927–1928 surrendered the British concessions at Hankou and Jiujiang and then in 1930 the Weihaiwei Leased Territory, which initially had been administered from Hong Kong. The Foreign Office even suggested giving up Hong Kong to conciliate Chinese nationalism, arguing that Britain no longer needed a formal colony to maintain its commercial interests in China. The Foreign Office furthermore opposed Clementi's plan to convert the leased New Territories into a permanent cession, which the governor thought would be vital for the future of Hong Kong, and which he believed was obtainable given China's fragmented state. The 1925–1926 strike in particular showed how much Hong Kong depended on China, for local business leaders had to use their connections with to import food and other provisions from Macau and Southeast Asia.

* * *

The strikes of the 1920s occurred around the same time as yet another debate over the *mui-tsai* system. What earlier had been mainly a local matter now became one of the longest and most intense British colonial-policy controversies of the interwar period. It was sparked by Clara Haslewood, the wife of a Royal Navy lieutenant commander, who learned about the practice only days after arriving in Hong Kong in August 1919 and then launched a campaign there and later in Britain against "child slavery" (Hoe, 1991: 232–246; Pedersen, 2001). In Britain, the campaign involved women's and workers' groups calling attention to the "Little Yellow Slaves under the Union Jack," and members of parliament and religious leaders. Even Colonial Secretary Winston Churchill, who had previously defended the system, in February 1922 promised the House of Commons that it would be ended within one year. Similar debates occurred in the Straits Settlements and elsewhere in Malaya (Leow, 2012).

Slave-girls carrying children

Figure 5 "Slave girls" (*mui-tsai*) carrying children,
ca. 1920 (courtesy of Tim Ko)

British activists made the *mui-tsai* system an imperial and international issue. But this debate was also very much a Chinese one – not only about slavery, labor, and gender, but about being Chinese in a modern world (Yuen, 2004: 101; Pomfret, 2008: 194). Because the system had been banned (though never enforced effectively) in China after the 1911 revolution, no one now could claim it was still a legitimate Chinese custom. Formed in August 1921, the Hong Kong Anti-Mui-Tsai Society soon had more than one thousand members. Its organizing committee comprised almost entirely Chinese Christians, many of them from the YMCA and YWCA, with help from local labor unions. The two Chinese members of the Legislative Council, Lau Chu Pak and Ho Fook, responded by forming the Society for the Protection of Mui Tsai, supported by the Tung Wah Hospital and Po Leung Kuk committees. Like many colonial officials, Lau and Ho took the anti-*mui-tsai* campaign as an attack on the respectability of the Po Leung Kuk and on Hong Kong's Chinese elite in general. They argued that critics were mainly foreigners who did not understand the system, and many colonial officials made the same argument (Pedersen, 2001: 172–173).

Local Chinese women, many of them Christians, played an active role in the anti-*mui-tsai* movement, offering an alternate view of Chinese custom and culture (Smith, 1981; Wong, 2003: 158–162). Among them was Fok Hing-tong, a cofounder of the YWCA (which published one of Hong Kong's first women's magazines) and the wife of Ma Ying Piu. These women were part of a nationwide program of Christian-led reform, not just in the treaty ports and other urban areas but across China (Dunch, 2001). Likewise, Christian or not, the members of the Anti-Mui-Tsai Society were members of a much larger movement for "women's emancipation" in China (Chin, 2012).

The controversy abated temporarily with the passing of the Female Domestic Service Ordinance in 1923, which Lau and Ho reluctantly supported. But it was revived after the Canton government banned all forms of slavery in March 1927 and cancelled deeds for the sale or transfer of *mui-tsai*. Reorganized, the Anti-Mui-Tsai Society declared in October 1928 that conditions in Hong Kong had become even worse. Yet Governor Clementi insisted there was no evidence that the number of *mui-tsai* had increased and the system could not be abolished without alienating the Chinese population, especially as long as it continued to exist in China, where the laws against it were not being enforced (Miners, 1987: 170–172). When in 1929 the Legislative Council passed an amendment requiring *mui-tsai* to be registered and paid wages, many Chinese resented being stigmatized for having one. Even though the Mui Tsai Ordinance was passed in 1930 and in 1938 the government made it compulsory to register all adopted girls, the system lasted much longer; some cases were reported as late as the 1970s. And with the escalating conflict between China and Japan in the late 1930s, it is hardly surprising that the *mui-tsai* issue began to fade from the limelight.

* * *

If the *mui-tsai* debate divided Hong Kong people, the Japanese threat united them in "newly energised ideas of nationalism" (Fok, 1990: 118). Hong Kong people had stood "together with the homeland" by participating in China's National Salvation Movement since the beginning of the Sino–Japanese conflict in the late 1920s (Lu, 2014). After Japan invaded China in July 1937, Hong Kong became a crucial source of arms for the Chinese war effort. Until the Japanese took Canton in October 1938, ammunition and supplies purchased overseas entered China each month via the Kowloon–Canton Railway, and then to other regions via the Canton–Hankow Railway or on foreign steamships. Hong Kong factories produced wartime supplies such as helmets and gas masks. Local merchants formed societies to support the Chinese war effort, including the Chinese Merchants Relief Association and the Chinese Women's Relief Association. Xu Dishan, head of the Chinese Department at the University of Hong Kong, was president of the local branch of the All-China

Figure 6 Film stars Ng Cho-fan and Leung Sheung-yin at fundraising event for Chinese war effort, February 1939 (courtesy of Tim Ko)

Resistance Association of Writers and Artists (Chan Lau, 1990: 267). Actors and other celebrities helped raise funds to support the war effort.

As it had during the Taiping Rebellion and after the 1911 revolution, Hong Kong became a haven for Chinese refugees – this time those fleeing the Japanese invasion. The population grew by about 500,000 from 1937 to 1940, becoming a "torrent" after 1939 and hitting a prewar peak of 1,800,000 in 1941, more than double that of 1931 (Leeming, 1977: 3). Refugees strained the colony's resources, but they also meant more workers for local industries, while land sales generated more government revenues. Many Chinese private and public institutions either evacuated to Hong Kong or set up local branches, among them the Bank of China and the Communications Bank. Chinese entrepreneurs brought not only capital but entire factories, dismantled and then reassembled in Hong Kong. Chinese dignitaries also took refuge in Hong Kong in those tense years. They included Soong Mei-ling, wife of Chiang Kai-shek; her brother T. V. Soong, former minister of finance in the Chinese government and later its minister of foreign affairs; and her sister Soong Ching-ling, Sun Yat-sen's widow, who moved the headquarters of her China Defence League to Hong Kong.

As during the revolutionary activities at the turn of the century, the colonial government had to remain neutral in the conflict between China and Japan. It rejected requests from the Chinese members of the Legislative Council to send relief money to China and turned down the Chinese government's request to arm local Chinese to help the war effort. Yet it could not afford to alienate its Chinese subjects by suppressing activities supporting the resistance. The government thus turned a blind eye to the efforts by the Communists and the Nationalists, which operated more or less unfettered. The Communists' Eighth Route Army opened a local office and a news agency to promote the war effort, while the Nationalists published newspapers and issued their own propaganda. In any case, concerns about neutrality eased in September 1939, when Britain declared war on Germany for invading Poland. Even though Britain was officially neutral in the conflict with Japan, with both nations now at war the local Chinese and British communities joined in common cause to support the war efforts in Europe and China.

When the Japanese attacked Hong Kong on December 8, 1941, Chiang Kai-shek sent three battalions to march on Hong Kong, though by the time they approached it was already too late: Governor Mark Young surrendered to Lieutenant Sakai Takashi on Christmas Day. Although the defense of Hong Kong lasted much longer than the Japanese had expected, the Japanese had been fighting in China for several years and could always count on reinforcements from across the border. The rapid loss of Hong Kong to Japan angered many Nationalist officials who had sent their families and money to the supposed safety of colonial Hong Kong. Still, the war saw some fruitful cases of Sino–British cooperation involving Hong Kong. The British Army Aid Group, a genuinely Hong Kong enterprise led by a professor at the University of Hong Kong, worked with the Nationalists from their wartime capital at Chongqing, and with the Communists' East River Column guerrillas in the New Territories and across the border in Guangdong and Guangxi. The British even relied on the East River Column to manage the New Territories after the war until they could handle the situation themselves (Chan, 2009: 95–106).

By early 1943, as the war began to favor the Allies, the British became determined to retain Hong Kong after the war. That summer they established in London the Hong Kong Planning Unit, led from 1944 by David MacDougall, who had escaped shortly after the Japanese invasion. Li Shu-fan, a well-known surgeon who escaped into Free China and then to London, assured the Colonial Office and the Foreign Office that most Chinese elites would prefer British rule over Chinese rule after the war. By mid-1945, Prime Minister Winston Churchill realized that Chiang could not try to recover Hong Kong without support from the United States, which now considered the continuation of European colonialism in Asia vital to its own interests.

It is tempting to read this as British overconfidence. Yet many options were discussed within the Colonial Office and the Foreign Office. Though with hindsight they may seem fanciful, these included returning the New Territories to China and then leasing them back, giving up all of Hong Kong, and making it an Anglo–Chinese condominium administered by the British. This is also very much a Chinese story. Encouraged by American president Franklin Delano Roosevelt (whose grandfather had been a partner in an American firm that traded in South China in the 1840s and whose mother had lived in Hong Kong), Chiang Kai-shek hoped to use the war to recover Hong Kong and end both the humiliating "unequal" treaties and the practice of extraterritoriality whereby foreigners, usually in the treaty ports, were tried by their own courts.

In mid-1942, Chiang's government approached Britain to return Hong Kong or at least the New Territories. Chiang asked his ambassador to Britain, Wellington Koo, to investigate the possibility. The timing seemed right: even Churchill and the Colonial Office conceded that Hong Kong might not remain a British colony after the war. In late 1942, the discussions began for abolishing extraterritoriality and revising the status of the New Territories. But Chiang's plan was shelved due to last-minute intervention from Koo, who realized that if the Chinese scuppered a new treaty with Britain because of the New Territories, they might miss the chance to win back the concessions in China proper that the

British were prepared to surrender (Whitfield, 2001: 85–106; Snow, 2003: 142–148).

As victory loomed, Roosevelt wanted Chiang to accept the surrender of almost all Japanese forces within China, including Hong Kong. Roosevelt had promised at the Cairo Conference in November 1943 to help Chiang recover Hong Kong if he in turn agreed to help Mao Zedong's Communists fight the Japanese. The British had other plans. They did not want to cause any trouble with Chiang and Roosevelt, but they intended to take back what they considered to be their own territory. Although Chiang was convinced he could count on American aid against the Communists after the war, he never knew exactly how much the United States would support any effort to recover Hong Kong. Despite pressure from within his government to recover Hong Kong or at least accept the Japanese surrender, Chiang preferred that Hong Kong be liberated by the British than by the Communists. In the end, Rear Admiral Cecil Harcourt accepted the Japanese surrender on behalf of Britain and China on September 16, 1945, in the presence of a Chinese military official and an American one. Instead of recovering Hong Kong, four years later Chiang Kai-shek would end up on Taiwan.

* * *

Hong Kong's postwar recovery was remarkably swift, thanks to the interim military administration and to the resilience and resourcefulness of Hong Kong people. The interim regime, which managed the colony for eight months, provided emergency food supplies, set price controls, and restored the fishing industry. By November 1945, the economy had recovered so well that controls were lifted and free markets restored. Several months later, trade had resumed to more than half of its prewar level. The colony became the main base for British commercial and industrial interests in East Asia, for preserving Britain's world-power status, and for maintaining prestige and morale (particularly after the humiliating loss of Hong Kong, Singapore, and Malaya to Japan in 1941–1942). Hong Kong gained even greater strategic importance in the late 1940s as the center for British commercial operations in China, especially after many British firms moved there during the civil war between the Communists and the Nationalists.

Equally important for this extraordinary recovery and growth was the chaos in China following the war and then during the civil war, which helped swell Hong Kong's population to 1 million by early 1946. Another million would come from 1946 to the mid-1950s, an average of three hundred per day. Hong Kong's industry was revived by an influx of Chinese entrepreneurs, especially textile spinners from Shanghai. From 1947 to 1949, almost all major Shanghai firms moved to Hong Kong, not only building upon the colony's earlier industrial base but expanding it. These textile industrialists, already experienced in working with foreigners in Shanghai, brought larger and more modern factories (Wong, 1988: 42–78). This gave the colony a significant economic head start over the rest of East Asia, much of which was being decolonized.

Even before the Communist victory in October 1949, the British realized they would have to tread carefully: trying to keep Hong Kong without alienating China (though this lesson had been partly learned in the 1920s and 1930s) and trying to stay neutral in the Communist–Nationalist struggle (this too had been learned in the 1911 revolution and in 1937–1941 before the Japanese invasion). Mark Young, who had surrendered to the Japanese in December 1941 and returned as governor after the war, hoped that Hong Kong might eventually become a city-state within the British Commonwealth. But he also realized the need to maintain good relations with China. So did Alexander Grantham, who replaced Young in July 1947 and saw only two options for Hong Kong: remain a British colony or return to China. Grantham's opposition to Young's plans for municipal reform derived partly from his conviction that he understood China better and partly from his experience in Hong Kong during the 1920s and 1930s (Tsang, 1988: 183–210).

Most British officials realized by late 1948 that the Communists would win and British relations with China would have to change. The question became no longer if, but when the Chinese would want Hong Kong back and how they would go about it. This explains why the British strengthened their garrison so substantially. Losing Hong Kong would hurt British prestige in Southeast Asia, especially after the independence of India, Burma, and Ceylon. Keeping it could be a good way to get support from the United States. With an insurgency in Malaya and the impending Communist victory in China, holding on to Hong Kong became of great psychological importance.

There were some tense moments. In April 1949, Communist batteries on the Yangzi River shelled a British warship, the *Amethyst*, killing the ship's captain and more than twenty other men, and humiliating both the Royal Navy and Britain. Several months later, the colonial government cracked down on local Communist activities and passed special public security legislation giving the governor wide powers. But the Communists seemed not to threaten British commercial interests in China, and the British were more worried about communists elsewhere: in Malaya, where an anticolonial guerrilla campaign lasted until the mid-1950s. More concerned with defeating the Nationalists, Mao Zedong considered Hong Kong a domestic matter to be handled later. Mao, who often insisted that Hong Kong was not a priority or even a concern and once referred to Hong Kong as a "wasteland of an island," reportedly told a British journalist in 1946 that he was not interested in reclaiming Hong Kong, and that as long as the British did not mistreat the colony's Chinese residents he would not let Hong Kong harm Sino–British relations.

Mao's nonchalant attitude notwithstanding, Hong Kong had been immensely useful to his Communists throughout the civil war. In 1947, they established the Central Hong Kong Bureau, which in early 1949, became the Central South China Bureau. Through the New China (Xinhua) News Agency, the Communists spread propaganda within Hong Kong, in China, and among overseas Chinese communities. They trained cadres in the safety of colonial Hong Kong and tried to recruit members from local schools and factories. In November 1948, the head of the local New China News Agency branch assured the British that a new Communist government would not bother Hong Kong and would even allow the colonial government to provide refuge to Nationalist leaders. By January 1949, Mao had decided not to worry about reclaiming Hong Kong or Macau. The Communists thus reassured the British they would not try to recover Hong Kong after they took power, ordering their troops not to cause too much trouble as they approached the border in mid-October. Another new era had begun – for China and for its colonial neighbor.

4 Hong Kong and Communist China

Who would have thought it possible? A Communist victory that helped end Britain's historically favored position in China also enabled Hong Kong to remain a British colony. Had Chiang's Nationalists won the civil war, they most likely would have tried to recover Hong Kong. Yet a Communist government that promised to help end capitalism and imperialism worldwide not only tolerated but even encouraged colonialism in Hong Kong. Far from ending Hong Kong's colonial status, the establishment of the People's Republic of China on October 1, 1949, gave it new prominence – in East Asia, in the British Empire, and across the globe. Despite being separated by the "Bamboo Curtain," Hong Kong and China were probably more useful to each other during this period than any other, especially in the final two decades.

Although the Communists insisted they were not interested in recovering Hong Kong, some British diplomats and policy makers assumed the colony would have to be surrendered. Instead, the Communist victory brought new talent and resources. Entrepreneurs and capitalists fled to Hong Kong and quickly invested in manufacturing (especially cotton textile production),

Figure 7 Lo Wu border crossing, ca. 1960 (courtesy of Tim Ko)

construction, and shipping, while fleeing workers provided cheap labor. Compared with the draconian and sometimes disastrous policies that characterized the first decades of the PRC, the new government's attitude toward Hong Kong remained consistently rational and sophisticated. Shortly after the establishment of the PRC, Foreign Minister Zhou Enlai told Qiao Guanhua, head of the local branch of the New China News Agency, that Hong Kong was a problem "left behind by history." Although China would not try to recover Hong Kong yet, Zhou explained, that did not mean "abandoning" it or "withdrawing" (in Mark, 2017: 38).

Soviet leader Josef Stalin once urged Mao Zedong to take Hong Kong because it was full of "imperialist agents" (in Goncharov, Lewis, and Xue, 1993: 40). Mao and his comrades, especially Zhou, realized that a British Hong Kong, however embarrassing, could be of great use, as it had been for more than a century. The New China News Agency conducted both "overt and covert" operations and united front activities in Hong Kong (Chu, 1999 and 2010: 41–57). Remittances from overseas Chinese offered valuable foreign exchange to help rebuild China's postwar economy, while the colony could be used for importing goods that China could not yet produce or obtain from its Russian and European allies, including heavy machinery and pharmaceuticals. As "the city of last resort" (Goodstadt, 2018: 187), Hong Kong enabled the mainland's socialist economy to interact with overseas trading and financial centers, often with the help of local "patriotic capitalists."

Hong Kong's survival depended on maintaining a good relationship with the PRC, especially the authorities in Guangdong. Retaining Hong Kong became a key economic interest and shaped British policy toward China (Clayton, 1997: chapter 5). The colonial government thus tried hard not to provoke the Chinese government. It avoided the matter of Hong Kong's colonial status and uncertain future, even though there was always a sense that 1997 (the end of the New Territories lease) mattered. The Hong Kong authorities persuaded the British government not to use the colony's radio station for spreading anticommunist propaganda, knowing it might lead to retaliation from the Chinese government. The colonial government also tolerated pro-Beijing secondary schools, even while it was concerned about them – especially after the 1967 riots, when teachers and students from such schools played an active role in the disturbances and their science laboratories were used for making bombs (Lau, 2013).

Culturally, the 1949 revolution helped make Hong Kong a new space. The colony became a base for prominent scholars and intellectuals who had fled from China. Among them were Luo Xianglin, an expert on Hakka language and culture who worked in the University of Hong Kong's Chinese Department, and Qian Mu, a historian who with anticommunist philosopher Tang Junyi and economist Zhang Pijie cofounded New Asia College, which later became part of the Chinese University of Hong Kong. Maintaining this "Chinese identity in exile" became a way to save and revive Chinese culture (Chou,

Figure 8 Tourists at the Lok Ma Chau border with mainland China, 1968 (courtesy of Tim Ko)

2011: 15–49). The closing of China to the "Free World" also made Hong Kong a major tourist destination, where overseas visitors unable to visit mainland China could get a taste of Chinese culture and catch a glimpse of the Communist giant just across the border.

* * *

Not only was there no real change in the Communists' policy toward Hong Kong after their victory, they appreciated it even more after the Korean War that broke out in June 1950. Hong Kong became an even more important trading partner than before, helping China break the embargoes on weapons and strategic products imposed by the United States and the United Nations (Schenk, 2001: 41). Scarce goods such as gas, kerosene, and penicillin were smuggled in through Hong Kong. The colony also served as a listening post for China, just as it did for Britain and America. Shortly after the war began, Zhou Enlai ordered local senior cadres and the head of the New China News Agency to heed the official policy of leaving Hong Kong alone, reminding them of the colony's usefulness in circumventing the embargoes and dividing Britain and America in their China and East Asia policies. In 1951, Politburo member Peng Zhen explained that recovering Hong Kong would both be too difficult and cause problems in China's international relations. Better, he argued, to maintain the colony's status quo and use it to rebuild China's economy (Tang, 1992: 186).

The Korean War and the US and UN embargoes eventually led Hong Kong to shift from the entrepot trade to manufacturing, accelerating the pre–World War II trend of manufacturing products for Southeast Asian markets. Smuggling could be highly lucrative, but it was risky and unreliable. Switching from trade to manufacturing did not, however, mean losing reliance on China. The labor for this industrialization depended on immigrants from China. Although in May 1950, the Hong Kong government limited the number of immigrants from the mainland, by the end of the year, the influx had increased the colony's population to almost 2 million. Though in February 1951, the Chinese government began to control internal migration to Guangdong, which in turn lowered immigration to Hong Kong, by 1955, the colony's population had risen to approximately 2.5 million. What colonial officials had called the "problem of people" now became the "power of people" – thousands of Chinese who were willing to work hard and less willing to complain or demand reforms from the colonial government (Mark, 2007).

This does not mean the relationship between Hong Kong and the new PRC was always a smooth one. A tramway strike in December 1949 provoked by Guangdong authorities failed. But it showed the colonial government the new regime was a force to reckon with. In March 1952, a violent confrontation occurred between the Hong Kong police and protesting crowds after the government promised to stop a "comfort mission" from Canton on its way to care for victims of a recent fire in Kowloon. One protester was shot dead, more than one hundred arrested, and twelve deported. After some ten thousand sympathizers protested the shootings and local left-wing newspapers tried to stir up anti-British feelings, the government shut down the pro-Beijing newspaper *Ta Kung Pao* for six months.

Further complicating matters, the PRC on the mainland and the Republic of China (ROC) on Taiwan both claimed to be the legitimate government of China. Often more troubling for Hong Kong than the political situation across the border were the conflicting British and American policies toward the two new regimes. While Britain officially recognized the PRC in early January 1950, the United States continued to recognize Chiang's ROC. The Americans were determined to keep Taiwan from falling to the Communists, while the British assumed it would inevitably become part of the PRC. Hong Kong became a site where the "global Cold War" was "played out on a daily basis" (Mark, 2017: 39).

Hong Kong thus had to learn to coexist within this dangerously fluid space (Tsang, 1997b; Carroll, 2008). Throughout the early 1950s, the Nationalists conducted guerrilla raids on Communist-held coastal islands and searched and harassed foreign vessels, including British freighters. In April 1955, the *Kashmir Princess*, a chartered Indian airliner that was supposed to transport Zhou Enlai (now both foreign minister and premier) to the Bandung Conference, exploded after taking off for Jakarta from Hong Kong's Kai Tak Airport, killing eleven Chinese officials and foreign journalists. Although the Chinese government demanded that the Hong Kong authorities capture the Nationalist agents responsible for sabotaging the aircraft, the service technician at the airport who had been bribed to place the bomb escaped to Taiwan (Tsang, 1994). Zhou reportedly told Governor Alexander Grantham in October during his visit to Beijing that the Chinese government would tolerate Hong Kong as long as the British abided by several "rules of conduct": Hong Kong could not be used as an anticommunist base, no activities aimed at subverting the PRC would be allowed, and the colonial government would protect PRC representatives and organizations (Mark, 2004: 29).

In October 1956, a clash between pro-Nationalist and pro-Communist supporters over a Nationalist flag that had been removed from a public housing block left fifty-nine people killed within two weeks (the highest number in the history of Hong Kong social unrest) and more than four hundred hospitalized. Although there was no evidence that Nationalist agents had participated directly, the Chinese government accused Britain and Taiwan of colluding to destabilize the PRC. Zhou Enlai reminded the British that China did not want to cause trouble in Hong Kong but could easily do so. In his official report on the riots, Grantham tried to downplay the political nature of the conflict while showing that his administration was still in control of the situation. But he was well aware that this was more than a local, spontaneous conflict: "These are people who have fled from their homeland, and it is not surprising if their fate has engendered a sense of frustration and bitterness" (Grantham, 1957: i).

Such incidents were more the exception than the rule, however, and the governments of Hong Kong and China, like those of Britain and China – "the Cold War's odd couple" (Tsang, 2006) – learned to forge a remarkably pragmatic relationship. For the Communists, Hong Kong was "somewhere between foreign policy and domestic policy" (Tsang, 1997a: 69). They quickly renounced the old treaties with Britain, continuing to insist that Hong Kong was a domestic matter to be handled later. Australian journalist and longtime Hong Kong resident Richard Hughes once wrote that "Chiang Kai-shek's Nationalists denounced Hong Kong in the past more fiercely than Mao's Communists have done since" (Hughes, 1968: 16). The PRC government even contributed money to a massive housing-resettlement scheme in Hong Kong initiated after a huge fire in Shek Kip Mei, Kowloon, in December 1953 (Smart, 2006: 104).

* * *

Hong Kong remained useful to China well beyond the Korean War. After the catastrophic Great Leap Forward (1958–1962) and then through the Cultural Revolution (1966–1976), imports were financed greatly by foreign currency acquired through Hong Kong. In the 1960s, the PRC earned almost half of its hard currency through selling food and water to Hong Kong (Cheung, 2014). Governor Grantham claimed that more hogs were slaughtered in Hong Kong than anywhere in the world except Chicago, with 90 percent of them coming from China (Grantham, 1965: 172). The PRC also used Hong Kong to sell Chinese-made cheap goods in Southeast Asia markets, including canned goods, bicycles, radios, and sewing machines – all costing half as much as their Japanese equivalents. As before, Hong Kong people continued to send money, food, and other goods to their relatives on the mainland.

The Star Ferry Riots of April 1966 were mainly a local affair – a reaction against government corruption, crowded housing, extreme wealth gaps, and lack of political representation. Yet they had China roots. Refugees had driven the population from around 4 million in 1960 to almost 5 million, mostly during the Great Leap Forward and the three years of famine that followed. Some one hundred and fifty thousand refugees came in 1962 alone, and by 1964, almost five hundred thousand squatters lived in hillside shacks or rooftop huts. The

Figure 9 Hong Kong Island and Victoria Harbour from Tsim Sha Tsui, ca. 1965 (courtesy of Tim Ko)

riots began on April 4 when the police arrested a man protesting an increase in ferry fares. By April 8, one rioter had been killed, many more injured, and more than fourteen hundred arrested. The official inquiry commission insisted the riots had not been caused by economic, political, or social conditions, and instead blamed a local British activist, Elsie Elliot, for stirring up trouble by soliciting public opinion on whether the fare increase was acceptable. Still, its report began by explaining how Hong Kong's "major problem" was population growth, "both natural and in the form of immigrants from China" and how "the underlying insecurity of life in the Colony, resulting from international political and economic conditions, creates tensions which elsewhere would be more than sufficient cause for frequent disturbances" (*Kowloon Disturbances 1966*, 1967: 3–4, 6).

The 1967 riots are a very different story. They too have local roots, similar to those behind the 1966 riots. But the main cause was the Cultural Revolution in China, where young people known as Red Guards and other radicals tried to continue Mao Zedong's revolutionary struggle. Starting in early May 1967, a labor dispute at a factory in San Po Kong, Kowloon, led to more than six months of violence. Left-wing activists marched through the streets, fought with the police, and planted bombs. By the end of the year, at least fifty-one people were dead, eight hundred injured in riots and clashes with the police, and more than three hundred hurt by bombs. One of the worst conflicts occurred in July, in Sha Tau Kok, a border town divided into Chinese and British sectors, when five policemen were killed by villagers and local militia from the Chinese side. Sino–British relations reached their lowest point since 1949. Yet even after the *People's Daily* on June 3 called on Hong Kong people to launch a "vigorous" struggle against the "wicked" British imperialists, the British government confirmed that it would help China secure a seat in the United Nations.

Whereas both the PRC media and the local left-wing press had criticized the 1966 riots, in 1967, the Anti-British Struggle Committee enjoyed strong support in China, at least in the early phases. How could it not? After all, the struggle in Hong Kong was part of the PRC's worldwide fight against imperialism. On May 17, 1 million protesters marched past the British office in Beijing armed with posters demanding that the British leave Hong Kong and vowing to hang Prime Minster Harold Wilson. A mass rally the next day in Beijing drew one hundred thousand people, including Premier Zhou Enlai, Foreign Minister Chen Yi, and Public Security Minister Xie Fuzhi. In August, protesters attacked the British diplomatic mission in Beijing and set it on fire.

In the end, however, the PRC government helped keep the movement from becoming too powerful – rerouting supplies to Hong Kong after Red Guards

Figure 10 Protesters outside Government House, 1967 (courtesy of Tim Ko)

disrupted them and resisting demands from the Red Guards to overthrow Hong Kong's colonial and capitalist systems. Although the water supply from China had been reduced during the riots and Governor David Trench feared the Chinese government would not miss a "golden opportunity" to leave Hong Kong "waterless" – on October 1, China's national day, the PRC followed its annual tradition of honoring its agreement to provide water to Hong Kong around the clock (in Clayton, 2018: 174–175). Indeed, the colonial government was reasonably confident throughout the disturbances that they were caused by local activists rather than by the Chinese government.

It may not be too much of an exaggeration to say that the Chinese government was as responsible for ending the riots as the Hong Kong government was. Nor should this be surprising. The PRC leadership understood, for example, the value of Hong Kong's membership in the Sterling Area: after the Great Leap Forward, a large part of China's imports had been financed by the sterling it was able to acquire through Hong Kong. From 1963 to 1967, acquiring sterling paid for almost 30 percent of China's total imports (Goodstadt, 2005: 59–60). American intelligence services predicted in 1967 that the PRC would be unlikely to drive the British out of Hong Kong, if only for the foreign exchange the colony provided (Mark, 2017: 67). This explains why Zhou Enlai intervened to make sure food and other vital supplies continued to reach Hong Kong despite the chaos of the Cultural Revolution (Goodstadt, 2018: 197). Although the riots reshaped the local political landscape in ways that still affect Hong Kong today (Cheung, 2017), relations between Britain and China recovered relatively quickly. In 1972, the two established full diplomatic relations for the first time since 1950.

* * *

Of the three periods we have seen, this is the one when Hong Kong identity grew the fastest and became the strongest. A sense of local identity had existed from the late 1800s on, especially among wealthier and Western-educated Chinese. It became stronger after the 1911 revolution and even more so in the 1920s, when people in Hong Kong contrasted the stability there with the chaos in China. But it became especially powerful from the 1970s on, and surveys starting in the mid-1980s showed that many Hong Kong people identified primarily as "Hongkongese" rather than as Chinese. They were neither British nor Western, yet not Chinese in the same way PRC citizens were (Baker, 1995; Mathews 1997). Over these decades evolved a local Hong Kong pop culture – particularly in film, television, and music – in Hong Kong's own form of Cantonese and even exported across the border (Gold, 1995).

Several factors explain this growth in Hong Kong identity. Most people born there after 1950 had little personal experience of China. Usually children of immigrants who had fled after the 1949 revolution, they were less likely to identify with the mainland, most of all its communist government. Until the revolution, Hong Kong people had moved freely across the border. This changed in 1950, when the border became a restrictive and militarized barrier (Madokoro, 2012), causing them to identify more closely with Hong Kong. By the 1970s, most people in Hong Kong had come to see it as a permanent home. The very different political and economic systems also mattered, as did the fact that Hong Kong people were saved from the catastrophes of the PRC, especially the Great Leap Forward and the Cultural Revolution. The 1967 riots were also an important cause, convincing many that no matter how corrupt the colonial government could be, it was preferable to the one across the border.

The Hong Kong government played a vital role in creating this sense of local identity. The closing of the border led to a sense of isolation for many Chinese people, which the government was quick to exploit. In 1952, the Education Department formed a committee to consider the place of Chinese history, language, and literature in the local school curriculum. In November 1953, the committee recommended an emphasis on Chinese culture, against the emphasis on nationalism and patriotism that was being promoted in China and Taiwan. Generations of children thus grew up identifying as culturally but not politically Chinese – "Chinese identity in the abstract, a patriotism of the émigré" (Luk, 1991: 667–668). The Hong Kong Festival, started in the wake of the 1967 riots, the Keep Hong Kong Clean Campaign of the early 1970s, and even the fight against corruption and the establishment of the Independent Commission against Corruption in 1974 were also attempts to build a local identity.

Hong Kong's rising economic prosperity and closer connections with China mattered too. By the late 1970s, the differences between Hong Kong and PRC became even more pronounced and obvious. The reopening of the border caused many people to identify even less with China and more with Hong Kong. The backwardness of China grew more apparent, from firsthand experience obtained through personal visits and from accounts by both legal and illegal immigrants. Familial, regional, and cultural ties persisted, of course. But stereotypes of mainlanders as hicks and bumpkins thickened, and the gradual reintegration with the mainland only reinforced such impressions.

This strengthened Hong Kong identity did not, however, imply a lack of interest in China. On the contrary, the growth of Hong Kong identity often coincided rather than conflicted with many events related to China: protests against Japanese claims to the islands known to them as the Senkaku and to the

Chinese as the Diaoyu; China Week and "know the motherland" exhibits organized by university students; efforts in 1974 to make Chinese an official language; and increased and faster visits to China, thanks to better transport links. Much of this new interest was inspired by American president Richard Nixon's visit to China in February 1972, which signaled China's reopening to the outside world, and by China's rising power and status (evident in its admission to the United Nations in 1971), though impressions of China soured as people in Hong Kong learned more about the brutality and mayhem of the Cultural Revolution.

* * *

China's rising power helped determine the form of Hong Kong's decolonization, which was led by China rather than by Britain or by Hong Kong people. The initial signs of a change to the PRC government's longtime policy of ignoring Hong Kong's colonial status appeared in 1972, when its first ambassador to the United Nations, Huang Hua, clarified Hong Kong's political status as "a Chinese territory under British administration." Huang also requested that Hong Kong and Macau be removed from the UN's list of colonial territories, explaining that Hong Kong was an internal matter to be solved by the PRC government "when conditions are ripe." But initially this did not seem to mean much. In 1974, the PRC government rejected Portugal's offer to return Macau. In September 1978, a senior official in the Hong Kong branch of the New China News Agency admitted that the 1967 riots had been a mistake and that China should learn from Hong Kong and from industrializing countries.

By the late 1970s, however, Hong Kong investors had become concerned about taking new leases if the colonial government could not grant any new ones beyond 1997. Governor Murray MacLehose was thus happy to accept an official invitation to Beijing in March 1979 from Minister of Foreign Trade Li Qiang. With thousands of land leases in the New Territories due to expire three days before July 1, 1997, MacLehose wanted to use the visit to replace these leases with ones that would remain valid as long as Britain continued to administer the New Territories. To the British delegates' surprise, new Chinese leader Deng Xiaoping seized the initiative by mentioning the long-term future of Hong Kong. But he assured the governor that Hong Kong investors could "set their hearts at ease." MacLehose relayed this news when he returned to Hong Kong, but avoided mentioning that Deng had rejected his proposal and that the PRC planned to recover Hong Kong.

MacLehose's visit to Beijing created a temporary sense of relief in Hong Kong. Prime Minister Margaret Thatcher's visit in September 1982 had the opposite effect. For Thatcher failed to convince Deng to let Britain keep administering Hong Kong. When she insisted that the treaties between Britain and China could only be altered and not abrogated, and that Britain had a moral obligation to the people of Hong Kong, Chinese officials declared that the treaties were unequal and had been signed with the long-defunct Qing government. By the time Thatcher left Beijing, it was clear that China would try to recover Hong Kong in 1997.

Deng's determination to take back Hong Kong was never only about Hong Kong. Earlier versions of "one country, two systems" had failed as an experiment in Tibet in the 1950s, and been rejected as a proposal by Taiwan in the 1950s and the 1980s; Deng's new model had Taiwan in mind, with Hong Kong an example to show that it could work (Hung and Kuo, 2013). And the timing was right. On January 1, 1979, the United States ended its formal diplomatic relations with Taiwan and agreed to terminate their mutual defense treaty, lest it would violate the principle of "one China." Thus, in March 1981, the Chinese leadership decided to recover Hong Kong in 1997, but in a way that would enable it to help China's modernization. Not all Chinese leaders agreed that Hong Kong should be allowed to keep its economic and political systems, but Deng was adamant that Hong Kong and Taiwan were part of the same problem. Deng prevailed, and in January 1982, Premier Zhao Ziyang informed Lord Privy Seal Humphrey Atkins that the PRC had already made provisions for Hong Kong after 1997. In July 1982, Peng Zhen (who in 1951 had advised against taking Hong Kong) discussed the idea of reunifying Hong Kong, Macau, and Taiwan as "special administrative regions."

This change in PRC official thinking toward Hong Kong occurred as Hong Kong and China were building a symbiotic relationship that would eventually move manufacturing from Hong Kong to China and make the Pearl River Delta into an industrial center. From the late 1970s on, Hong Kong investment and business know-how helped China's economic reforms, while China provided land and labor for Hong Kong manufacturing and started to play a greater role in the colony's economy. Hong Kong manufacturers were eager to cut production costs by moving their factories to Guangdong, especially in the new Shenzhen Special Economic Zone, where businesses were keen to learn from their neighbors across the border. By the mid-1990s, Hong Kong firms had opened thousands of factories and plants in China, hiring 3 million workers in Guangdong alone and 5 million in China overall. Ninety percent of Hong Kong factories had moved to China, leaving manufacturing to count for less than 10 percent of Hong Kong's GDP.

The mid-1980s to the end of the colonial era in 1997 saw the maturation of this economic relationship, one that depended heavily on China's economic growth, particularly in Guangdong. Hong Kong facilitated China's

Figure 11 Pipeline supplying water from mainland China to Hong Kong, 1979 (Library of Congress Prints and Photographs Division)

modernization as a financier, trading partner, middleman, and facilitator (Sung, 1991: 16–28). The colony became the PRC's primary conduit for capital, modern technology, and management skills, providing almost one-third of its foreign exchange earnings. By 1986, Hong Kong was doing more business with China than with any other country. From 1977 to 1987, total exports from Hong Kong to China grew almost 260 times, domestic exports more than 500 times, and reexports more than 200 times. The colony's traditional entrepot status was also revived: in 1988, almost 70 percent of Hong Kong imports from China were then reexported.

Meanwhile, China used Hong Kong as a channel for market information and technology transfer, while businessmen and investors from nations without diplomatic relations with China did business with China in and through Hong Kong. Yet many Hong Kong people today forget the role China played in Hong Kong's modernization. China's economic reforms helped transform Hong Kong from a light industry center to a leading financial and service one. By 1985, Chinese investment in Hong Kong was estimated at US$6 billion In 1986, China was the third-largest investor in Hong Kong, after the United States and Japan. By 1994, China was investing more than twice as much as the United States and Japan combined. More than seventeen hundred Chinese companies were registered in Hong Kong, hiring more than fifty thousand people.

* * *

The last fifteen years of colonial Hong Kong were unusual in several ways, one being the cause for decolonization. The demand came not from local people, but from a government that had the power to recover Hong Kong. How the tables had turned since the 1840s! Far from a colonial embarrassment, Hong Kong had become more economically advanced than most independent countries. Apart from being a major financial center, by the end of British rule, it had the second-highest per capita GDP in Asia (after Japan), and had surpassed that of Britain, Australia, and Canada. The long decolonization process allowed Hong Kong people to become acquainted gradually with their new masters, and vice versa. But because the Chinese government claimed to represent the wishes of Hong Kong people, they were all but ignored in the Sino–British negotiations that would determine their future; Governor Edward Youde was allowed to participate only as a member of the British delegation. Most notably, rather than being granted independence as most colonies were, Hong Kong was turned over to a far more authoritarian government than the one that had ruled it for so long.

The negotiations took two years – longer than the Chinese wanted but shorter than what the British had in mind. The initial issues and obstacles were the Chinese side's demand that the British acknowledge PRC sovereignty over

Hong Kong, and Britain's hope to continue administering Hong Kong after 1997. The Sino–British Joint Declaration, signed on December 19, 1984, by Margaret Thatcher and Zhao Ziyang and ratified on May 28, 1985, listed the main terms of the agreement on Hong Kong's future political status. All of Hong Kong would revert to Chinese rule on July 1, 1997. Hong Kong would become a special administrative region of the PRC, with "a high degree of autonomy." Its social, legal, and economic systems would remain unchanged. Hong Kong would remain a free port, with no taxes paid to China. Rights and freedoms of speech, assembly, and religion would be preserved. The People's Liberation Army would not interfere in Hong Kong affairs. This "one country, two systems" arrangement would last for fifty years after 1997.

Contrary to Deng Xiaoping's expectations, the Joint Declaration did not arouse the kind of joy and excitement that accompanied decolonization else-where. While many people were relieved that a deal had finally been struck, opinion polls showed that most of the population preferred Hong Kong to remain a British colony. Eager for a smooth transition, the Chinese government tried to build a "broad united front" among the Hong Kong community: appeasing democratic politicians by promising self-government in the future and winning the allegiance of businesspeople by vowing to continue Hong Kong's capitalist system (Hung, 2010: 60–61). The Chinese side soon started drafting the Basic Law, the region's constitution that would go into effect on July 1, 1997. Here the PRC government had several goals: ensuring that any political changes in Hong Kong would fit what China wanted after 1997; making the Joint Declaration more palatable to Hong Kong people and the world; proving it was sincere about "one country, two systems" yet also showing that it would be in charge of Hong Kong's future; and winning the support of Hong Kong people, especially prodemocracy leaders such as Martin Lee and Szeto Wah, by including them on the drafting committee.

The law took almost five years to draft. The first draft, released in late April 1988 for a five-month consultation period, led to a torrent of public criticism for not providing room for representative government. Surveys in 1988 showed that more than half of the respondents believed that returning to Chinese rule would harm civil rights and individual liberty. The second draft, released in late February 1989 for an eight-month consultation, was also criticized, not only by liberal groups but even by moderate and conservative ones. The drafting process was then disrupted by the demonstrations in Beijing that ended in the Tiananmen Square Massacre on June 4, 1989, and then by the resignations of publisher and novelist Louis Cha and Anglican bishop Peter Kwong after martial law was imposed on May 20, and by the ejection of Martin Lee and Szeto Wah, the loudest advocates of democratization and the cofounders of the Hong Kong Alliance in Support of the Patriotic Democratic Movement in China.

The demonstrations in Tiananmen Square had been hopeful signs that China might become more democratic. After Premier Li Peng imposed martial law, more than five hundred thousand people – almost one-tenth of Hong Kong's population – marched in protest (and during a severe typhoon). Significantly, the largest protest in Hong Kong history up to then was not about Hong Kong but about China, though it was also an expression of fear and concern for Hong Kong's future. The Hong Kong Alliance in Support of the Patriotic Democratic Movement in China raised money through a huge pop concert and sent blankets, tents, and sleeping bags to the protesters in Beijing. Even conservative businesspeople showed their support, hoping that reform in China might speed up democratization in Hong Kong and thereby secure its future after 1997.

The brutal crackdown in Beijing on June 4 horrified people across the globe. But Hong Kong people had a special reason to worry: they understood that one point of the suppression at Tiananmen was to prevent a similar event from happening anywhere else in China. The result was the largest public protest in Hong Kong history – almost 1 million people, many wearing white and black (the traditional Chinese mourning colors) and from all parts of society, including pro-Beijing trade unionists, businesspeople, and even employees of pro-Beijing newspapers and the Bank of China. Some tried to force a run on local branches of PRC banks by withdrawing all their deposits. A group of Hong Kong tycoons attempted to offer Beijing HK$10 billion in return for self-rule for ten years after 1997. One proposal called for China to lease Hong Kong to the United Nations for one hundred years. Attitudes toward 1997 changed almost overnight, with a dramatic loss of faith in the PRC government and in confidence for Hong Kong's future. The stock market dropped by 25 percent, property values plummeted, and applications for immigration visas skyrocketed.

The Tiananmen Square Massacre was a defining moment in the Hong Kong–China nexus. Perhaps more than any event in Chinese history, it showed how tragedies in China could affect Hong Kong. For many people, it was a wake-up call for reflection – not only on their confidence in the Joint Declaration but on the very idea of "one country, two systems." Tiananmen was also a moment of monumental importance for the formation of local identity. It made many Hong Kong people feel more Chinese than ever, even while forcing them to look elsewhere. People had been leaving before and throughout the Sino-British negotiations in the early 1980s, but the scale and intensity increased dramatically after the Joint Declaration and especially after Tiananmen, when the colony saw a "gathering wave of emigration" (Wong, 1999: 136). Some sixty-six thousand people emigrated in 1992 alone.

Tiananmen strengthened Hong Kong identity more than anything since the signing of the Joint Declaration. Many people started to realize the difference between "cultural" China and "political" China – loving the culture and seeing themselves as ethnic Chinese, yet loathing the Communist regime. The massacre also led to an "explosion in Hong Kong's civil society" (So, 1999: 159): people became more interested in politics, reviving defunct student movements and founding new organizations. The massive turnout in the annual June 4 vigil commemorating the massacre over the past three decades attests to its relevance to the Hong Kong–China nexus, even after the vigil was prohibited in 2020 in the name of social distancing.

The new Bill of Rights enacted in June 1991, which the Chinese government argued violated the spirit of the Joint Declaration and threatened to repeal, did little to restore confidence. Nor did the British Nationality (Hong Kong) Act enacted in July 1990, which offered full British citizenship to fifty thousand Hong Kong people and their families without having to leave Hong Kong – partly because the PRC government insisted it would not recognize them as British nationals after 1997. Even less reassuring was the response of the Chinese government, which condemned Hong Kong people for sending money to the demonstrators and even accused them of trying to help overthrow the PRC government. Tiananmen reinforced Beijing's wariness of the subversive potential of the city and its vulnerability to overseas interests. Some officials described the Tiananmen protests as a Hong Kong–US plot. On July 11, Chinese Communist Party general secretary Jiang Zemin reminded Hong Kong people that "the well water does not interfere with the river water," warning them not to interfere in mainland politics. The PRC government purged several local Communist groups that had supported the demonstrators and had participated in the Hong Kong protests before and after the massacre.

Tiananmen made Hong Kong people distrust the PRC government even more than ever, creating a sense of anger, frustration, and helplessness evident in the diverse responses. It also led to years of distrust and suspicion between the Hong Kong and PRC governments. The situation only became worse when in October 1989, Governor David Wilson announced a plan to build a new airport and container port, the construction of which would extend almost ten years past the 1997 transition. The plan was widely seen as an attempt to restore confidence in Hong Kong's future, and even Wilson admitted as much. But the Chinese government condemned Wilson for not consulting it beforehand. As Jiang Zemin put it, "you invite the guests, but I pay the bill." The matter was not resolved until the end of June 1991, with help from British foreign secretary

Douglas Hurd and veteran diplomat Percy Cradock. According to the terms of the agreement, officially signed on September 3, Hong Kong would pay for the first part of the airport project; a PRC official would participate in the planning and construction; the British and Chinese foreign ministers would meet regularly; and Prime Minister John Major would visit Beijing, making him the first major Western leader to do so since Tiananmen.

The eleventh-hour political reforms of Hong Kong's last colonial governor, Chris Patten, led to several more years of friction. Patten aimed to widen the electoral base of the functional constituencies and strengthen representation in the Legislative Council. Although he was responding to widespread local demands for more reform, his "crash course in Western democracy" (Pepper, 1997: 695) was widely seen as an attempt to protect Hong Kong after 1997 while helping Britain withdraw honorably. The Chinese government claimed he had violated the terms of the Joint Declaration and demanded that he be replaced. Patten's reforms made him a hero in Hong Kong; the more the Chinese government criticized him, the more popular he became. Worried that the Hong Kong democracy movement might revive that in the mainland, Beijing assumed an even stronger stance against Patten's reforms. In July 1993, in the midst of the furor over Patten's proposed reforms, the PRC formed a preliminary working committee to build a "new kitchen" – the Chinese term for starting a new household but in this case a provisional government that would administer Hong Kong after 1997.

* * *

At midnight on July 1, 1997, Hong Kong became part of the PRC. Shortly before then, Charles, Prince of Wales, who led the British delegation to the handover ceremony, promised the people of Hong Kong that "we shall not forget you, and we shall watch with the closest interest as you embark on this new era of your remarkable history." Jiang Zemin, the first PRC leader ever to visit Hong Kong, declared that "Hong Kong compatriots have become true masters of this Chinese land" and that Hong Kong would enter a "new era of development." New chief executive Tung Chee-hwa, the first Chinese to administer Hong Kong in more than 150 years, proclaimed that "for the first time in history, we, the people of Hong Kong, will be master of our own destiny" and that "Hong Kong and China are whole again." In Beijing, more than twelve hundred miles away, one hundred thousand carefully selected guests watched President Jiang's handover speech on gigantic television screens in Tiananmen Square. Hong Kong was "home at last."

For the Chinese leadership, recovering Hong Kong was "a historic mission to erase a national disgrace" (Lau, 1997: 15). The slogan "Wash Away One

Hundred Years of Shame" was everywhere in China (somehow ignoring the first half-century of British rule). Recovery was also a major step toward China's adaptation to the outside world (Yahuda, 1997: 192). Above all, at least for Deng Xiaoping (who died that February and was unable to see his dream fulfilled), recovering Hong Kong was a chance to prove to the world (especially to Taiwan) that Beijing was sincere about the "one country, two systems" model. Although most people in China had not paid much attention to Hong Kong until then, the final countdown to 1997 was observed with great enthusiasm and fanfare. The historic nature and the political urgency of the transition were inscribed in the Hong Kong Clock installed in the middle of Tiananmen Square in 1994 – a "graphic reminder" (Yahuda, 1996: 94) to people on the mainland and in Hong Kong and both a "threatening gesture" and a "political timer" (Wu, 1997: 352, 354) warning Hong Kong people against using democracy as a pretext to subvert communism in China.

Reactions in Hong Kong ranged from pride to nostalgia and apprehension, expressed in a variety of ways. Artists and writers articulated their concerns about "living in the shadow of the future" through their work (Clarke, 2001: chapter 2). Crowds queued for hours to buy the last set of postage stamps bearing the portrait of Queen Elizabeth. Others applied for naturalization as British Dependent Territory Citizens. This would qualify them to apply for the British National (Overseas) Passport, which would not grant them the right to live in Britain but would enable them to travel without visas to many countries. One thing is certain, however: few Hong Kong people saw themselves as going home. For no matter how much China had changed, it was still very different from Hong Kong. Polls in January and May 1996 showed that only one-fifth of the young people surveyed considered mainlanders to be reliable, and more than three-quarters identified themselves first as Hongkongese rather than Chinese.

Yet many Hong Kong people do not realize how much confidence in their city's future had risen by early 1997. A survey in February showed that more than 60 percent of respondents were "optimistic" or "very optimistic," and more satisfied than ever before with the PRC government. Moreover, more than 60 percent (as opposed to around 40 percent in February 1993) preferred reunification with China rather than remaining a British colony or becoming independent (not that either was an option). Another survey revealed that public confidence was as high as before Tiananmen, still another that almost 75 percent believed Hong Kong would remain stable and prosperous after 1997, though surveys also found that many people were still worried about their personal freedom.

Some of this confidence was due to a last-minute charm offensive by the PRC government. In late 1995, Vice-Premier Li Lanqing promised that Chinese enterprises would not enjoy any special privileges in Hong Kong. The vice-director of the New China News Agency compared Hong Kong's economy to a big cake, insisting that such enterprises were in Hong Kong "not to divide the cake," but to make it "bigger and bigger, sweeter and sweeter." In April 1996, the PRC government invited Chief Secretary Anson Chan to a meeting in Beijing with Vice-Premier Qian Qichen, who praised Hong Kong's civil servants and urged them to stay on after 1997 (which Chan and many others indeed did). Qian also insisted that the elections for Hong Kong's chief executive would be transparent and fair, and that the candidates had to be acceptable to local people. As it had through the New China News Agency after 1949, in the years leading up to 1997, the Beijing government enlisted the support of local "patriotic capitalists."

Much of this confidence was also due to Hong Kong and China's growing economic interdependence – "Hong Kong in China" and "China in Hong Kong" (Pepper, 2008: 289–291). By the late 1980s, this relationship had helped make Hong Kong the world's third largest financial center behind London and New York. On the eve of 1997, almost one hundred thousand Hong Kong residents were working in mainland China, mostly in Guangdong but also in other cities such as Shanghai and Beijing. Hong Kong had become the largest investor in China, handling half of China's exports, almost 60 percent of its total foreign investment, and one-third of its exchange reserves. By 1997, Chinese investment in Hong Kong was probably as much as Hong Kong investment in China, with Chinese-funded enterprises controlling up to 25 percent of Hong Kong's major service industries. Not exactly home at last, but at least much closer together than any time since 1949.

5 Building a New Nexus

Decolonization is rarely an easy process. Even colonies that become independent nations without warfare or other forms of bloodshed usually face serious challenges. In this regard, Hong Kong's transition from colony to special administrative region was remarkably smooth. Where else in Asia was decolonization so peaceful and orderly? Where else was there so little hostility, let alone retribution, against foreign colonials and the locals who collaborated with them? Where else did most people see so little immediate difference in their daily lives? And where else did the political and economic systems remain so unchanged ? The very term chosen by the Chinese government for the resumption of sovereignty – "return" (*huigui*) – conveyed a "sentimental notion of homecoming" and made the process appear to be a natural one, indicating that the government had little intention of introducing any significant reforms (Law, 2018: 236).

The smoothness of this aspect of Hong Kong's decolonization should not surprise us, given how well Hong Kong and China coexisted from the early 1840s all the way to 1997. There are many other ways, however, to assess the twenty-four years since the reversion to Chinese sovereignty. Especially compared with the "miracle" of the 1970s and 1980s, economic growth has been "lacklustre," while rising income inequality has made life harder for many Hongkongers, especially workers (Wong, 2017: 101–106). Hong Kong's infamous "poverty in the midst of affluence" has been exacerbated by the government's hostility toward social expenditure (Goodstadt, 2013: 12). Corruption has reached the upper echelons of government. None of the first three chief executives served more than one term. Each of the first three administrations was dogged with scandal and controversy, and in early 2019, the fourth took Hong Kong into its worst political crisis ever. It seems almost an understatement to say that Hong Kong suffers from "social and institutional fractures" (Fong and Lui, 2018).

To be sure, not all of Hong Kong's problems can be blamed on reintegration with the mainland. Most are "postcolonial hangovers" (Hampton, 2016: 211–218) – political and economic legacies of the colonial period, among them the power of the business elite, especially from the property sector, and a conservative economic doctrine that prevents the SAR from expanding its welfare and housing policies. Restrictions on freedom of assembly, expression, and association aimed at suppressing political activism in British Hong Kong have remained in effect in Chinese Hong Kong. All former colonies have had teething problems, and the Hong Kong version of "one country, two systems" is after all "an institutional innovation without precedent" (Yep, 2013:7). Moreover, "learning how to belong to a nation" (Mathews, Lui, and Ma, 2008) after being a colony for so long is not easy. But Hong Kong's unique postcolonial status has exacerbated many of these problems. Reintegration has worsened the city's housing crisis, for example. And although universal suffrage is enshrined in the Basic Law, it has been effectively shelved.

The Hong Kong and Beijing governments have failed to persuade skeptical Hongkongers that reintegration is not recolonization. Even before 1997, scholars, journalists, lawmakers, and businesspeople predicted Hong Kong would go from "colony to colony" (Scott, 1995). Such prognostications followed through the handover and a new term has emerged: "mainlandization." This refers not only to Beijing's attempts to curb the "high level of autonomy" promised in the Sino–British Joint Declaration and the Basic Law, but also to the promotion of Mandarin over Cantonese (and English), the influx of mainland tourists and residents, and mega infrastructure projects such as the Hong Kong–Zhuhai–Macau Bridge, designed to fold Hong Kong even more closely into the "Greater Bay Area" comprising Guangdong, Hong Kong, and Macau.

Ironically, tensions between Hong Kong and the mainland have become worse than during the colonial era – not just in the early post-1997 years but further into the two-plus decades since, the Occupy Central/Umbrella Movement of 2014, and especially during the anti-extradition protests that began in early 2019. The Beijing government is convinced that Hong Kong people fail to grasp the importance and significance of the "one country" part of "one country, two systems," while many Hong Kong people want the SAR to remain "a system apart" (Cartledge, 2017) and resent Beijing for trying to make it "just another Chinese city" (though exactly what that means is rarely specified). This also is about much more than politics: for many Hongkongers, China's sovereignty has become "an existential and identity-laden crisis" (Vucovich, 2020: 8).

For many Hong Kong people, what separates the SAR most from the mainland are its "core values." Top among these is the rule of law, which although only selectively applied in the colonial era, has become a way of distinguishing Hong Kong from the mainland, and thus Hongkongers from mainlanders (Jones, 2018: 123). Language too has become an important form of self-identification. Despite government efforts to promote the use of Mandarin while demoting that of English, many Hong Kong people, especially youth, see it as a second language almost as foreign as English. Which language to use has thus become "a choice laden with political implications and identity symbolism" (Lam-Knott, 2018: 99–100, 103).

Although the SAR government has tried various forms of "patriotic education" to construct new identities and "transform hearts and minds" (Cheng, 2019: 177), these efforts have "not only failed but also backfired" (Yew and Kwong, 2014: 1109). In summer 2012, students, parents, and teachers forced the government to shelve a proposed "moral and national education" curriculum. Without any political affiliations or links to opposition politicians, students formed their own organization, Scholarism, whose leader, fifteen-year-old Joshua Wong, would play an important role in the Occupy Central/Umbrella Movement and in local politics thereafter. Whereas the colonial authorities encouraged identification with Chinese culture to counter the revolution across the border, the Beijing government's promotion of patriotism to justify deferring universal suffrage has pushed some young Hongkongers against the idea of China "even on a cultural level" (Veg, 2015: 70–71).

The resumption of Chinese sovereignty has had an important effect on informal relations between Hong Kong and the mainland. Most mainland immigrants adapt to their new environment and community by learning Cantonese, finding jobs (often low-paying ones), and sending their children to local schools (Luk, 2018: 35). Yet only a decade into the handover, becoming part of China seemed to make Hong Kong more parochial than before; this "siege mentality" saw mainlanders as threats to the region's status quo (Lee, 2008: 276). In January 2012, after an outspoken mainland professor criticized Hong Kong people for discriminating against mainlanders and refusing to identify as Chinese, calling them "bastards" and "running dogs for the British colonialists," angry locals responded by organizing a campaign that likened mainland tourists and immigrants to swarms of locusts.

Current Hong Kong–mainland interactions must be contextualized within the strategic position of Beijing in global politics and Beijing's geopolitical considerations. Local confidence in the notion of "one country, two systems" involves a sense of superiority of Hong Kong institutions and practices vis-à-vis those in the mainland. Yet the self-assurance of many locals has faded with the rapid growth of China's economy over the past four decades. Adapting Hong Kong practices to the logic of mainland operations is now the name of the game for benefiting from reintegration. But the trend of becoming more parochial is also related to the growing uneasiness of China within the global community: despite the Beijing's regime enthusiasm for recognition from the international community, relationships with its neighbors in the region and with key players in world politics have been uneasy in recent years.

The souring of the Hong Kong–mainland relationship has also manifested itself in sport. In 2018, during the World Cup qualifying rounds, Hong Kong fans booed the PRC national anthem after the Chinese Football Association released a poster referring to the Hong Kong team as "Hong Kong, China" and warning the Chinese team to hold its guard against a multiethnic Hong Kong team of players with "black skin, yellow skin, and white skin." Chanting "We are Hong Kong," many Hong Kong fans held banners saying "The Power of Hong Kong" and "Hong Kong Is Not China." When the Hong Kong fans were then prohibited from booing the national anthem, in the next match, they held signs saying "boo" in English. Mainland fans waved the national flag and held banners declaring "Hong Kong Independence Is Poison" – the words "independence" and "poison" being homophonic in both Mandarin and Cantonese.

Government officials and their supporters frequently point to these as examples of how Hong Kong people have failed to embrace the motherland. But it has not always been ordinary people who have fanned the flames of anti-mainlander sentiment. It was the government and its supporters who lit the first match. Shortly after the handover, the new Legislative Council issued ordinances restricting the procedures for applying for right-of-abode (permanent residency) status. When the Court of Final Appeal in 1999 supported legal challenges against the new ordinances, the government warned that the court's ruling would extend eligibility to some 1.6 million potential immigrants from the mainland and strain resources. The Standing Committee of the National People's Congress (NPC), which reserves the right to interpret the Basic Law, sided with the Hong Kong government. Critics accused the government of manipulating figures and exaggerating effects on housing, employment, and public health to create a climate of fear and encourage anti-immigrant sentiments. Pro-Beijing newspapers, however, supported the Standing Committee's decision, while the chairman of the pro-establishment Democratic Alliance for the Betterment of Hong Kong urged the government to find the "best possible way" to keep the potential immigrants from coming.

* * *

Despite doom-and-gloom predictions that Beijing might kill its golden goose, the new SAR's earliest challenge had little to with the reversion to Chinese sovereignty. This was the Asian financial crisis, brought on by currency devaluation in Thailand, only one day after the end of British rule in Hong Kong. It led to a drop in the Hong Kong stock market and in property values, unemployment, and a recession from which the SAR did not fully recover until late 2000. The most serious crisis of the early postcolonial years, however, *was* related to reintegration. In 2001, Chief Executive Tung Chee-hwa tried to introduce an anti-sedition bill, endorsed by Beijing and in accordance with Article 23 of the Basic Law, which gives the Hong Kong government the right to "prohibit any act of treason, secession, sedition, subversion against the Central People's Government" and to prohibit local political organizations from having contact with foreign ones. After large public demonstrations both for and against the proposed legislation, in early 2003, Tung's government announced that the Legislative Council would vote on the bill in July.

The bill might well have passed, but in March, the region was struck by severe acute respiratory syndrome (SARS). By the end of June, when Hong Kong was removed from the World Health Organization's list of SARS-affected areas, almost two thousand people had been diagnosed and three hundred had died. Even before the world learned that the Beijing government was concealing the true number of SARS patients, the Hong Kong authorities were under siege for not recognizing the disease earlier and for downplaying reports that the infection was coming from the mainland. With mainland authorities refusing to acknowledge the extent and severity of SARS, Hong Kong became the "de facto epicentre" of the outbreak (Loh, 2004: 236).

The SARS crisis affected Hong Kong more directly than any since the Tiananmen Square Massacre, revealing the political, social, and medical consequences of reintegration with China. It shattered confidence in both governments. On July 1, the sixth anniversary of Hong Kong's return to Chinese sovereignty, more than five hundred thousand people staged the "largest indigenous social movement" in Hong Kong history (Ma, 2007: 210), forcing Tung to drop his proposed security bill. Although, unlike in June 1989, this demonstration was motivated mainly by events and forces within Hong Kong, it was also aimed at the Beijing government for its lack of transparency and it inability to handle the SARS crisis. Although the main theme of the protest was opposition to Article 23, it expanded to a range of other appeals and demands, including universal suffrage in the upcoming chief executive and Legislative Council elections.

Just as SARS had important political repercussions, so did the massive protest it helped provoke (Lo, 2008: 151–184). It was a slap in the face of the Hong Kong government and the Beijing government, which began to intervene more directly in local affairs. In April 2004 the NPC's Standing Committee ruled out universal direct elections for chief executive in 2007 and the Legislative Council in 2008. On July 1, the seventh anniversary of the transition, hundreds of thousands protested the decision. The Beijing government also began to groom a new generation of "local tycoons" (Cheung, 2012: 336–337) and to blame anti-SAR government activities on "foreign intervention" and collusion between "hostile foreign forces" and opposition politicians.

* * *

The Mainland and Hong Kong Closer Economic Partnership Agreement, introduced by the Beijing government in late June 2003 as a "gift" during the SARS recession (and, some would say, to increase economic reliance on the mainland), indeed helped revive Hong Kong's economy. But greater integration also moved more jobs from Hong Kong to the mainland and sped the flow of capital from the mainland, driving up property prices and the cost of living (Hung, 2010: 69). One part of the agreement, the Individual Visit Scheme, which allowed mainlanders to visit Hong Kong individually for leisure rather than for business or as part of tour groups, became one of the main causes of tension. Although the scheme benefited Hong Kong's economy, for many locals it opened the door to far too many tourists, driving up rents in areas popular with tourists and changing their character. Businesses eager to profit from big-spending tourists did little to help the situation. In January 2012, more than one thousand people protested at the flagship store of Italian fashion house Dolce & Gabbana in Tsim Sha Tsui, Kowloon, after security guards banned locals from taking photos outside the shop but allowed mainland tourists to do so.

Conflicts have often been even worse on the border. The Individual Visit Scheme increased cross-border "parallel trading" by mainlanders who buy their goods in Hong Kong and then resell them at higher prices across the border. Local residents complained that this resulted in price increases and shortages of goods such as infant milk powder, which tourists were purchasing in large amounts to capitalize on worries in the mainland about tainted goods. In mid-September 2012, during a rally against parallel trading, a scuffle broke out at the MTR station in Sheung Shui, the last stop before the Lo Wu station on the border. Organizers of this "Reclaim Sheung Shui" movement claimed that parallel traders were disrupting the normally peaceful life of this small town, vowing to "liberate" it. Although the government limited how much formula each person could take across the border, some legislators urged it to regulate the number of mainland tourists.

The Individual Visit Scheme also enabled pregnant mainland women to travel to Hong Kong to give birth, which would qualify their children to right of abode. Hongkongers complained that this was depriving local residents of hospital beds and natal care. In October 2011, one thousand mothers organized a protest against birth tourism. Tensions became so bad that in February 2012, a group of Hongkongers placed a full-page newspaper advertisement branding mainland tourists as "locusts." The pressure grew so great that the government eventually agreed to prohibit mainland women from giving birth in Hong Kong.

* * *

By 2012, Hong Kong had become known as a "city of protest," its marches and demonstrations even becoming tourist sites (Dapiran, 2017: 5). Then in autumn 2014 came Occupy Central and the Umbrella Movement, which lasted just under eighty days. Although the idea to "Occupy Central with Love and Peace" had been first outlined in early 2013 by Benny Tai, a law professor at the University of Hong Kong, it was put into action almost spontaneously after another decision by the Beijing government to delay universal suffrage. On August 31, the NPC Standing Committee decreed that although universal suffrage for the chief executive election would be introduced in 2017, only suitable candidates vetted by a nominating committee would be allowed to run. Activists, most of them born and educated after 1997, blocked roads in the Admiralty part of Central, the city's main financial center. Their professed aim was to pressure the Beijing government into giving Hong Kong an electoral system that would meet "international standards" of universal suffrage. The name "Umbrella Movement" took root when on September 28 protesters used umbrellas as shields against police tear gas. A massive display of civil disobedience followed, with more "occupations" in Causeway Bay on Hong Kong

Island and Mong Kok in Kowloon. Not only the largest civil disobedience campaign in Hong Kong history, the Umbrella Movement was "the largest protest campaign on Chinese soil involving the occupation of public space" since the demonstrations at Tiananmen (Lee and Chan, 2018: 1).

Unlike the demonstrations in 1989 before and after Tiananmen, or the annual vigil commemorating the massacre, the Umbrella Movement did not "engage in rhetoric about the future of the nation" (Veg, 2015: 55). Still, like the annual July 1 protest marches, including the momentous one in 2003, it targeted the Hong Kong and Beijing governments, which in turn condemned the movement as illegal, secessionist, and engineered by "foreign forces." Mainland authorities blocked out news coverage there and suppressed support by arresting sympathizers. And even though the movement had a specific goal – universal suffrage – it was "preceded and underpinned by discursive elaborations of local identity" (Veg, 2017: 339). These localist dimensions were expressed in the movement's slogans, including "Take Back Our Future" and "Fight for the Place You Love and Where You Belong."

Eventually, the Hong Kong government used civil court injunctions to clear the occupied areas peacefully and end the movement. But observers predicted – correctly as it turned out – that Hong Kong people, especially younger ones, would not only become more politically active but would use more radical means to demand universal suffrage and greater autonomy for their city, and that the movement would "likely deepen social cleavages and send the city toward an uncertain future" (Yuen, 2015: 49). The Umbrella Movement produced new forms of localism and even demands for independence – including through organizations such as Hong Kong Indigenous, Youngspiration, and the Hong Kong National Party – leading to "unprecedented polarization in Hong Kong, engulfing state and society in ever hardening antagonism" (Lee, 2019: 3).

This bitterness became even more apparent during the so-called Fishball Revolution in Mongkok in February 2016, when a clash between passers-by and hygiene officers trying to remove unlicensed food vendors erupted into violent protests led by Hong Kong Indigenous. Even more than the Umbrella Movement itself, these localist sentiments alarmed mainland authorities. In late 2015, Wang Zhenmin, dean of the Tsinghua University Law School in Beijing (and in 2016 appointed the legal chief of Beijing's liaison office in Hong Kong), argued that two of the "deep-rooted" issues facing Hong Kong were its inability to accept that it was part of the motherland and the urgent need to fully implement "one country, two systems" and the Basic Law.

* * *

Figure 12 Occupy Central protesters, Admiralty, October 2014 (photo by Tim Ko)

Nothing since 1997 has tested the relationship between Hong Kong and the mainland more than the extradition bill introduced by Chief Executive Carrie Lam in February 2019, and the year of social unrest that followed. The bill would have allowed fugitives to be extradited to several jurisdictions, including the mainland. But many Hongkongers (including from the pro-Beijing camp) were worried about any possibility of Hong Kong people being sent to face trial in a jurisdiction with such a weak human rights record. Although the bill did not include political crimes, it was widely seen as an attempt to suppress dissent. Given how so many Hong Kong people abhor the mainland's legal and political systems, introducing the bill was "a catastrophic miscalculation" (Vucovich, 2020: 9).

The government's refusal to withdraw the bill led to a series of protests: a march on June 9 that reportedly drew 1 million people, a clash between protesters and police on June 12, and then a march of 2 million on June 16 – by far the largest in Hong Kong history. These were followed by protests against police brutality (mainly the use of pepper spray and tear gas) and against the police for not preventing attacks by mobs, allegedly with police connivance and not only on protesters but on bystanders not involved with the protests. Even pro-government politicians admitted they had underestimated how much Hong Kong people distrusted mainland China: the main slogan of the protests, "Oppose Being Sent to China" (*faan sung zong*) was also a homophone for "oppose being sent to die."

The scope of the protest movement soon widened to "five demands and not one less": withdrawal of the extradition bill; the resignation of Carrie Lam and the introduction of universal suffrage; retraction of the word "riot" to describe earlier protests; independent investigations of police brutality; and withdrawal of criminal charges against the protesters. After the annual protest march on July 1, a group of protesters stormed the Legislative Council building and vandalized the council chambers, including the city's emblem. Protests and clashes with the police occurred almost every weekend.

While the Umbrella Movement protesters failed to convince the general public that their peaceful methods were appropriate, the more radical protesters in 2019 found a surprising high level of support from Hong Kong society, even when they turned to tactics such as throwing petrol bombs. Protests in August that paralyzed the city's airport for five days ended when police moved in after the protesters surrounded and roughed up two men they believed to be mainland undercover agents. The mainland media had not covered the Hong Kong protests until then. But they did now, and the two men became heroes – especially one who happened to be a journalist for the *Global Times*, a tabloid controlled by the Chinese Communist Party through the *People's Daily*.

Figure 13 Anti-extradition protest at Hong Kong International Airport, August 2019 (photo by Catherine Monteil)

Figure 14 Anti-extradition pamphlet aimed at travelers, August 2019

Even more than the Umbrella Movement, the anti-extradition protests had
a strong localist dimension – including their own song, "Glory to Hong Kong,"
which became known as the Hong Kong national anthem. The movement's
main slogan, "Liberate Hong Kong, Revolution of Our Times," became popular
in mid-July, having first been used in 2016 by activist Edward Leung Tin-kei

while running for Legislative Council. Though many people used the slogan to mean liberating the city from Lam's government, she cited its popularity as proof that the essence of the movement had shifted from anti-extradition to anti-China.

Although Lam agreed on September 4 to withdraw the bill in October, protesters continued to insist that all five demands be met. They also became more extreme in their tactics. In September, Annie Wu Suk-ching, daughter of the founder of the Maxim's catering empire, called protesters "brainwashed zombies" who had been spoiled by their parents. Wu blamed the protests on the Education Bureau for not teaching Hong Kong youth about their Chinese identity and for not promoting national education. Radical protesters responded by vandalizing outlets run by Maxim's, including Starbucks, and those of mainland-linked (sometimes only allegedly) firms, naming their actions "renovation" and "decoration." Restaurants and shops were soon labeled according to their political inclinations: "blue" (pro-government and pro-Beijing) or "yellow" (anti-government and anti-Beijing, yellow being the color of the umbrella that symbolized the Umbrella Movement).

On October 1, the seventieth anniversary of the founding of the PRC, protesters held a "national grief" march. Some fought with the police, set fire to the national flag, and burned portraits of Carrie Lam and President Xi Jinping. Protesters also vandalized MTR stations and parts of the MTR line. Although Lam's government officially withdrew the bill on October 23, the protests continued. In November began a five-day battle on the campus of the Chinese University of Hong Kong, in the New Territories, with students, staff, and alumni (and many people without any links to the university) vowing to "safeguard Chinese University and resist police brutality." The subsequent two-week-long siege of Polytechnic University in Kowloon turned this campus too into a battleground. Miraculously, neither conflict involved any fatalities.

Hong Kong also became entangled in the US–China rivalry that had simmered for decades but came to a boil after Donald Trump became president in 2017 and soon after launched a trade war against China. During the protests of June 2019, some protesters waved American flags. Several opposition leaders visited the United States that year, urging the US Congress to pass the proposed Hong Kong Human Rights and Democracy Act, which would allow the United States to sanction anyone believed responsible for eroding Hong Kong's autonomy from Beijing. The act was approved with bipartisan support and signed into law in November 2019, though some academics and members of the US State Department (and the former American consul general in Hong Kong) argued that it would only punish Hong Kong and hurt its prospects for autonomy. If previous charges of collusion with "enemy agents" and intrusion by "hostile" foreign powers were often unsupported, this time Beijing had its proof.

* * *

By the end of 2019, Hong Kong appeared to be "on the brink" (Wasserstrom, 2020) and a "city on fire" (Dapiran, 2020). The Law of the People's Republic of China on Safeguarding National Security in the Hong Kong Special Administrative Region, passed in summer 2020 during the COVID-19 crisis (Burns, 2021: 87–88), signaled that Beijing had lost patience with both local activism and the Hong Kong government's inability to suppress it. Earlier that year, the government had already prohibited protests in the name of social-distancing restrictions. In mid-April, Luo Huining, Beijing's top official there, called for a national security law to be passed as quickly as possible. Many Hong Kong people had a "rather weak concept of national security," Luo explained, and "the anthill eroding the role of rule of law" had to be removed. The law was passed unanimously by the NPC Standing Committee on June 30, and only that night were the Hong Kong public and local officials (supposedly, even the chief executive) informed of its content. Obviously aimed at the 2019 protests, it gives the central government wide powers to crack down on a range of political crimes, including "secession, subversion, terrorism, and colluding with foreign countries." The most commonly used word in public reactions when the law was first announced was "chilling."

Given that most countries have national security laws and most Hong Kong people knew such a law would come sooner or later, why were they so concerned? The law appears to give Beijing unlimited freedom to interfere in Hong Kong's legal affairs. It mandates the central government to establish a new security committee within the Hong Kong government, with an advisor appointed by Beijing and a national security office with an extensive network of mainland officers based in Hong Kong, handling cases according to mainland law and free from the jurisdiction of the local authorities. The central government, rather than the Hong Kong government or judiciary, will determine how the law should be interpreted, while mainland law will take priority over Hong Kong law. The new law also gives the chief executive the authority to appoint judges to hear national security cases, which activists fear will jeopardize judicial autonomy. "Making Hong Kong China" now appears to mean more than scaling back human rights and the rule of law: it has become a clash of two incompatible political and legal cultures (Davis, 2020).

Although the new law states that the rights of suspects and defendants will be respected, many Hongkongers worry about the harsh and often arbitrary legal practices prevalent in the mainland. Both central and SAR authorities insist the law affects only "a tiny number of criminals who seriously endanger national security." But it applies to all Hong Kong residents and even more: foreigners who support independence, for example, or call for sanctions on the central government may be prosecuted upon entering Hong Kong or mainland China. The two governments claim the law will restore stability and guarantee prosperity. But critics – even some from conservative business circles who are worried it will weaken Hong Kong's position as a financial center – have called it the "end of Hong Kong."

* * *

The new law aims to remake the Hong Kong–mainland nexus into one more favorable to the interests of Beijing, allowing the SAR only a "truncated autonomy" (Lo, 2020). The rebuilding process does not stop there. On March 11, 2021, the NPC approved a resolution ensuring that only "patriots" can run Hong Kong. The move was necessary, officials maintained, to achieve "democracy with Hong Kong characteristics." The central government has also restricted the SAR's electoral system so that only those deemed sufficiently "sincere" and patriotic may serve or run; four lawmakers were ousted in 2020 alone, and politicians and civil servants are now required to take loyalty oaths. And where will these patriots come from? From the powerful, pro-establishment Democratic Alliance for the Betterment of Hong Kong? Or perhaps from the new Bauhinia Party, named after the SAR's official flower and emblem, and founded by mainland businesspeople who have moved to Hong Kong and been alarmed by the recent turmoil?

What is clear, however, is that, as in most societies, inculcating patriotism will begin with the young. In February 2021, the Education Bureau issued a circular explaining how it was the responsibility of schools to promote national security education – "a part of, and inseparable from, national education." There is nothing unique about using education to strengthen national identity. What stands out in the proposed curriculum is how many references it makes to the nation and how few to the SAR. Among the "fundamentals" of national security education, it explains, are to "develop in students a sense of belonging to the country, an affection for the Chinese people, a sense of national identity." Aimed at the 2019 protests, the curriculum promises to "enable students to become good citizens who have a sense of national identity, show respect for the rule of law and abide by the law." Schools should thus adopt a "multi-pronged and co-ordinated" approach to promoting national security education "holistically," even through subjects such as biology and geology. Some parents worry their children will become "little pinks" – young xenophobic Chinese nationalists.

* * *

Is this the end of Hong Kong? Doomsayers have been predicting the territory's death since 1949, but especially in the years leading up to 1997. Assuming China's economic development continues and that Beijing remains willing to support Hong Kong, there seems little reason to doubt that the SAR will remain a thriving metropolis, a vibrant financial center, and a gateway for China and the rest of the world. It will continue to be a destination for mainland Chinese seeking economic opportunities and for tourists. But this is likely to be the end of a relationship between Hong Kong and China that endured for more than 150 years. For the first time since the mid-1800s, Hong Kong is no longer a haven for dissidents from the mainland. Rather, it has become a place activists have started to flee *from*, especially after the passing of the national security law. The new law has made many Hongkongers feel less secure, less confident in the rule of law, and less part of the nation.

Although Hong Kong may continue to contribute to China's economic growth and benefit from it, the region is unlikely to be a base for reforming China politically, as it was in the late 1800s and early 1900s, and as some Hongkongers hoped it would after 1997. It is also unlikely again to become a site of protest – not only the "rebel city" of 2019 (Ibrahim and Lam, 2020) – but perhaps not even one of peaceful demonstrations. Until 2020, when the government banned such events, on each anniversary of the Tiananmen Square Massacre thousands of protesters, among them many mainlanders, held peaceful vigils. Hong Kong was the only place in China where the events of 1989 could be commemorated, evidence of how the territory still retained a degree of political freedom and even the ability to influence reform movements on the mainland (Cheung, 2011: 719; Hung and Ip, 2012: 519).

Given how quickly everything has moved since the introduction of the new security law, it may be premature to make any more predictions. Yet one thing is certain: the new nexus will take work on all sides. Activists will have to learn to operate within the framework allowed by Beijing. They will also have to realize that Beijing is unlikely to accept that not all demands for greater autonomy are calls for independence. Neither Hong Kong nor Beijing officials can assume, as Deng Xiaoping did, that all Hong Kong people will embrace being part of China. And Beijing will have to offer Hong Kong people more than promises of stability and prosperity. It will also have to admit that they are not solely to blame for the SAR's "deep-rooted" issues.

Bibliography

Abe, K. (2018). *Chinese Middlemen in Hong Kong's Colonial Economy.* London: Routledge.

Baker, H. D. (1995). Social change in Hong Kong: Hong Kong man in search of majority. In D. Shambaugh, ed., *Greater China: The Next Superpower.* Oxford: Oxford University Press, pp. 212–225.

Benedict, C. (1996a). *Bubonic Plague in Nineteenth-Century China.* Stanford, CA: Stanford University Press.

Benedict, C. (1996b). Framing plague in China's past. In G. Hershatter, E. Honig, J. N. Lipman, and R. Stross, eds., *Remapping China: Fissures in Historical Terrain.* Stanford, CA: Stanford University Press, pp. 27–41.

Bergère, M.-C. (1989). *The Golden Age of the Chinese Bourgeoisie, 1911–1937. Trans.* Janet Lloyd. Cambridge: Cambridge University Press.

Bickers, R. (2020). *China Bound: John Swire & Sons and Its World, 1816–1980.* London: Bloomsbury.

Burns, J. P. (2021). Public policy and learning from SARS: Explaining COVID-19 in Hong Kong. In S. L. Greer, E. J. King, E. M. da Fonseca, and A. Peralta-Santos, eds., *Coronavirus Politics: The Comparative Politics and Policy of COVID-19.* Ann Arbor: University of Michigan Press, pp. 86–104.

Carroll, J. M. (2006). Colonial Hong Kong as a cultural-historical place. *Modern Asian Studies*, 40(2), 517–543.

Carroll, J. M. (2007). *A Concise History of Hong Kong.* Lanham, MD: Rowman & Littlefield/Hong Kong: Hong Kong University Press.

Carroll, J. M. (2008). Contested colony: Hong Kong, the 1949 revolution, and the "Taiwan problem." In D. Kerr, Q. S. Tong, and S. Wang, eds., *Critical Zone 3.* Hong Kong: Hong Kong University Press/Nanjing: Nanjing University Press, pp. 75–93.

Carroll, J. M. (2005). *Edge of Empires: Chinese Elites and British Colonials in Hong Kong.* Cambridge, MA: Harvard University Press.

Carroll, J. M. (2009). A national custom: Debating female servitude in late nineteenth-century Hong Kong. *Modern Asian Studies*, 43(6), 1463–1593.

Cartledge, S. (2017). *A System Apart: Hong Kong's Political Economy from 1997 until Now.* Docklands, VIC: Penguin Australia.

Chan, M. K. (1995). All in the family: The Hong Kong–Guangdong link in historical perspective. In R. Y-W. Kwok and A. Y. So, eds, *The Hong Kong–Guangdong Link: Partnership in Flux.* Armonk, NY: M. E. Sharpe, pp. 31–63.

Chan, M. K. (1990). Labour vs. Crown: Aspects of society-state interactions in the Hong Kong labour movement before World War II. In E. Sinn, ed., *Between East and West: Aspects of Social and Political Development in Hong Kong*. Hong Kong: Centre of Asian Studies, University of Hong Kong, pp. 132–146.

Chan, M. K. (1997). The legacy of the British administration of Hong Kong: A view from Hong Kong. *China Quarterly*, 151, 567–582.

Chan, S. (2009). *East River Column: Hong Kong Guerrillas in the Second World War and After*. Hong Kong: Hong Kong University Press.

Chan Lau, K. (1990). *China, Britain and Hong Kong, 1895–1945*. Hong Kong: Chinese University Press.

Chan Lau, K. (1999). *From Nothing to Nothing: The Chinese Communist Movement and Hong Kong, 1921–1936*. New York: St. Martin's Press.

Chappell, J. (2018). Maritime raiding, international law and the suppression of piracy on the South China coast, 1842–1869. *International History Review*, 40(3), 473–492.

Cheng, E. W. (2019). Hong Kong's hybrid regime and its repertoires. In C. K. Lee and M. Sing, eds., *Take Back Our Future: An Eventful Sociology of the Hong Kong Umbrella Movement*. Ithaca, NY: Cornell University Press, pp. 167–191.

Cheung, G. K. (2017). How the 1967 riots changed Hong Kong's political landscape, with the repercussions still felt today. In M. H. K. Ng and J. D. Wong, eds., *Civil Unrest and Governance in Hong Kong: Law and Order from Historical and Cultural Perspectives*. New York: Routledge, pp. 63–75.

Cheung, P. T. Y. (2012). The changing relations between Hong Kong and the mainland since 2003. In W. Lam, P. L. Lui, and W. Wong, eds., *Contemporary Hong Kong Government and Politics*. Hong Kong: Hong Kong University Press, pp. 325–348.

Cheung, P. T. Y. (2011). Who's influencing whom? Exploring the influence of Hong Kong on politics and governance in China. *Asian Survey*, 51(4), 713–38.

Cheung, S.-K. (2014). Reunification through water and food: The other battle for lives and bodies in China's Hong Kong policy. *China Quarterly*, 220, 1012–1032.

Chin, A. S. (2012). *Bound to Emancipate: Working Women and Urban Citizenship in Early Twentieth-Century China and Hong Kong*. Lanham, MD: Rowman & Littlefield.

Choi, H. S. H. (2017). *The Remarkable Hybrid Maritime World of Hong Kong and the West River Region in the Late Qing Period*. Leiden:Brill.

Chou, G. A. (2011). *Confucianism, Colonialism, and the Cold War Chinese Cultural Education at Hong Kong's New Asia College, 1949–63*. Leiden: Brill.

Chu, C. Y. (2010) *Chinese Communists and Hong Kong Capitalists: 1937–1997*. New York: Palgrave Macmillan.

Chu, C. Y. (1999). Overt and covert functions of the Hong Kong branch of the Xinhua News Agency, 1947–84. *Historian*, 62(1), 31–46.

Chung, S. P. (1998). *Chinese Business Groups in Hong Kong and Political Change in South China, 1900–25*. London: Macmillan.

Clarke, D. (2001). *Hong Kong Art: Culture and Decolonization*. London: Reaktion.

Clayton, D. (1997). *Imperialism Revisited: Political and Economic Relations between Britain and China, 1950–54*. Basingstoke, UK: Macmillan.

Clayton, D. (2018). The roots of regionalism: Water management in postwar Hong Kong. In G. C. Luk, ed., *From a British to a Chinese Colony? Hong Kong before and after the 1997 Handover*. Berkeley: Institute of East Asian Studies, University of California Berkeley, pp. 166–185.

Cohen, P. A. (1987). *Between Tradition and Modernity: Wang T'ao and Reform in Late Ch'ing China*. Cambridge, MA: Council on East Asian Studies, Harvard University.

Dapiran, A. (2017). *City of Protest: A Recent History of Dissent in Hong Kong*. Docklands, VIC: Penguin Australia.

Dapiran, A. (2020). *City on Fire: The Fight for Hong Kong*. Melbourne: Scribe.

D'Arcy-Brown, L. (2012). *Chusan: The Forgotten Story of Britain's First Chinese Island*. Kenilworth, UK: Brandram.

Darwin, J. (1997). Hong Kong in British decolonisation. In J. M. Brown and R. Foot, eds., *Hong Kong's Transitions, 1842–1997*. Basingstoke: Macmillan, pp. 16–32.

Davis, M. C. (2020). *Making Hong Kong China: The Rollback of Human Rights and the Rule of Law*. Ann Arbor, MI: Association for Asian Studies.

Dunch, R. (2001). *Fuzhou Protestants and the Making of a Modern China 1857–1927*. New Haven, CT: Yale University Press.

Eitel, E. J. (1895). *Europe in China: The History of Hong Kong from the Beginning to the Year 1882*. Hong Kong: Kelly and Walsh.

Faure, D. (1997). Reflections on being Chinese in Hong Kong. In J. M. Brown and R. Foot, eds., *Hong Kong's Transitions, 1842–1997*. London: Macmillan, pp. 103–120.

Faure, D. (2003). *Colonialism and the Hong Kong Mentality*. Hong Kong: Centre of Asian Studies, University of Hong Kong.

Fletcher, J. (1978). The heyday of the Ch'ing order in Mongolia, Sinkiang and Tibet. In J. K. Fairbank, ed., *The Cambridge History of China*, vol. 10, *Late Ch'ing*, part 1. Cambridge: Cambridge University Press, pp. 351–408.

Fok, K. C. (1990). *Lectures on Hong Kong History: Hong Kong's Role in Modern Chinese History*. Hong Kong: Commercial Press.

Fong, B. C. H., and T.-L. Lui, eds. (2018). *Hong Kong 20 Years after the Handover: Emerging Social and Institutional Fractures after 1997*. Cham, CH: Palgrave Macmillan.

Fung, C. M. (2005). *Reluctant Heroes: Rickshaw Pullers in Hong Kong and Canton, 1874–1954*. Hong Kong: Hong Kong University Press.

Gerth, K. (2003). *China Made: Consumer Culture and the Creation of the Nation*. Cambridge, MA: Harvard University Asia Center.

Gerth, K. (2020). *Unending Capitalism: How Consumerism Negated China's Communist Revolution*. Cambridge: Cambridge University Press.

Gillingham, P. (1983). *At the Peak: Hong Kong between the Wars*. Hong Kong: Macmillan.

Girardot, N. J. (2002). *The Victorian Translation of China: James Legge's Oriental Pilgrimage*. Berkeley: University of California Press.

Gold, T. B. (1995). Go with your feelings: Hong Kong and Taiwan popular culture in Greater China. In D. Shambaugh, ed., *Greater China: The Next Superpower*. Oxford: Oxford University Press, pp. 255–273.

Goncharov, S., J. W. Lewis, and L. Xue. (1993). *Uncertain Partners: Stalin, Mao and the Korean War*. Stanford, CA: Stanford University Press.

Goodstadt, L. F. (2018). Economic relations between the mainland and Hong Kong, an "irreplaceable financial center." In G. C. Luk, ed., *From a British to a Chinese Colony? Hong Kong before and after the 1997 Handover*. Berkeley: Institute of East Asian Studies, University of California Berkeley, pp. 186–213.

Goodstadt, L. F. (2013). *Poverty in the Midst of Affluence: How Hong Kong Mismanaged Its Prosperity*. Hong Kong: Hong Kong University Press.

Goodstadt, L. F. (2005). *Uneasy Partners: The Conflict between Public Interest and Private Profit in Hong Kong*. Hong Kong: Hong Kong University Press.

Grantham, A. (1957). *Report on the Riots in Kowloon and Tsuen Wan October 10th to 12th, 1956*. Hong Kong: Government Printer.

Grantham, A. (1965). *Via Ports: From Hong Kong to Hong Kong*. Hong Kong: Hong Kong University Press.

Hamilton, P. E. (2020). *Made in Hong Kong: Transpacific Networks and a New History of Globalization*. New York: Columbia University Press.

Hampton, M. (2016). *Hong Kong and British Culture, 1945–97*. Manchester University Press.

Hase, P. H. (2008). *The Six-Day War of 1899: Hong Kong in the Age of Imperialism*. Hong Kong: Hong Kong University Press.

Hayes, J. (2006). *The Great Difference: Hong Kong's New Territories and Its People, 1898–2004*. Hong Kong: Hong Kong University Press.

Hayes, J. (1984). Hong Kong Island before 1841. *Journal of the Hong Kong Branch of the Royal Asiatic Society*, 24, 104–142.

Hoe, S. (1991). *The Private Life of Old Hong Kong: Western Women in the British Colony*. Hong Kong: Oxford University Press.

Hong Kong Labour Department. (1939). *Report by the Labour Officer Mr. H. R. Butters on Labour and Labour Conditions in Hong Kong*. Hong Kong: Noronha.

Hughes, R. (1968). *Hong Kong: Borrowed Place, Borrowed Time*. London: André Deutsch.

Hung, H. (2010). Uncertainty in the enclave. *New Left Review*, 66, 55–77.

Hung, H., and I. Ip. (2012). Hong Kong's democratic movement and the making of China's offshore civil society. *Asian Survey*, 52(3), pp. 504–527.

Hung, H., and H. Kuo. (2013). "One country, two systems" and its antagonists in Tibet and Taiwan. In R. Yep, ed., *Negotiating Autonomy in Greater China: Hong Kong and Its Sovereignty before and after 1997*. Copenhagen: Nordic Institute of Asian Studies, pp. 179–206.

Ibrahim, Z., and J. Lam, eds. (2020). *Rebel City: Hong Kong's Year of Water and Fire*. Singapore: World Scientific Publishing.

Jones, C. A. G. (2015). *Lost in China? Law, Culture and Identity in Post-1997 Hong Kong*. Cambridge: Cambridge University Press.

Jones, C. A. G. (2018). A ruling idea of the time? The rule of law in pre- and post-1997. In G. C. Luk, ed., *From a British to a Chinese Colony? Hong Kong before and after the 1997 Handover*. Berkeley: Institute of East Asian Studies, University of California Berkeley, pp. 112–140.

Kowloon Disturbances 1966: Report of Commission of Inquiry. (1967). Hong Kong: Government Printer.

Kwan, C. N. (2020). "Putting down a common enemy": Piracy and occasional interstate power in South China during the mid-nineteenth century. *International Journal of Maritime History*, 32(3), 697–712.

Kwan, D. Y. K. (1997). *Marxist Intellectuals and the Chinese Labor Movement: A Study of Deng Zhongxia (1894–1933)*. Seattle: University of Washington Press.

Lam-Knott, S. (2018). Government and language in Hong Kong. In G. C. Luk, ed., *From a British to a Chinese Colony? Hong Kong before and after the 1997 handover*. Berkeley: Institute of East Asian Studies, University of California Berkeley, pp. 77–111.

Lau, C. K. (1997). *Hong Kong's Colonial Legacy: A Hong Kong Chinese's View of the British Heritage*. Hong Kong: Chinese University Press.

Lau, T. (2013). State formation and education in Hong Kong: Pro-Beijing schools and national education. *Asian Survey*, 53(4), 728–753.

Law, W. S. (2018). Reunification discourse and Chinese nationalisms. In G. C. Luk, ed., *From a British to a Chinese Colony? Hong Kong before and after the 1997 handover*. Berkeley: Institute of East Asian Studies, University of California Berkeley, pp. 236–258.

Lee, C. K. (2019). Take back our future: An eventful sociology of the Hong Kong Umbrella Movement. In C. K. Lee and M. Sing, eds., *Take Back Our Future: An Eventful Sociology of the Hong Kong Umbrella Movement*. Ithaca, NY: Cornell University Press, pp. 1–33.

Lee, F. L. F., and J. M. Chan. (2018). *Media and Protest Logics in the Digital Era: The Umbrella Movement in Hong Kong*. Oxford: Oxford University Press.

Lee, L. O. (2008). *City between Worlds: My Hong Kong*. Cambridge, MA: Harvard University Press.

Leeming, F. (1975). The earlier industrialization of Hong Kong. *Modern Asian Studies*, 9(3), 337–342.

Leeming, F. (1977). *Street Studies in Hong Kong: Localities in a Chinese City*. Hong Kong: Oxford University Press.

Leow, R. (2012). "Do you own non-Chinese *mui tsai*?" Reexamining race and female servitude in Malaya and Hong Kong, 1919–1939. *Modern Asian Studies*, 46(6), 1736–1763.

Lethbridge, H. J. (1971). A Chinese association in Hong Kong: The Tung Wah. *Contributions to Asian Studies*, 1, 144–158.

Lethbridge, H. J. (1978). The evolution of a Chinese voluntary association in Hong Kong: The Po Leung Kuk. In H. J. Lethbridge, *Hong Kong: Stability and Change; A Collection of Essays*. Hong Kong: Oxford University Press, pp. 71–103.

Lo, S. S. (2008). *The Dynamics of Beijing–Hong Kong Relations: A Model for Taiwan?* Hong Kong: Hong Kong University Press.

Lo, S. S. (2020). Hong Kong in 2020: National security law and truncated autonomy. *Asian Survey*, 61(1), 34–42.

Lo, S. S. (2007). The mainlandization and recolonization of Hong Kong: A triumph of convergence over divergence with mainland China. In J. Y. S. Cheng, ed., *The Hong Kong Special Administrative Region in Its First Decade*. Hong Kong: City University of Hong Kong Press, pp. 179–231.

Loh, C. (2004). Lessons learned. In C. Loh and Civic Exchange, eds., *At the Epicentre: Hong Kong and the SARS Outbreak*. Hong Kong: Hong Kong University Press, pp. 235–250.

Loh, C. (2010). *Underground Front: The Chinese Communist Party in Hong Kong.* Hong Kong: Hong Kong University Press.

Lu, Y. (2019). *Crossed Paths: Labor Activism and Colonial Governance in Hong Kong, 1938–1958.* Ithaca, NY: Cornell East Asia Program, Cornell University.

Lu, Y. (2014). In the wake of political intervention: British Hong Kong and the Lingnan macroregion. *Frontiers of History in China*, 9(3), 449–471.

Luk, B. H. (1991). Chinese culture in the Hong Kong curriculum: Heritage and colonialism. *Comparative Education Review*, 35(4), 650–668.

Luk, G. C. (2022). Accommodating foreigners in a littoral borderland: The lower Pearl River Delta during the Opium War. *Modern China*, 48(1), 197–228.

Luk, G. C. (2018). Straddling the handover: Colonialism and decolonization in British and PRC Hong Kong. In G. C. Luk, ed., *From a British to a Chinese Colony? Hong Kong before and after the 1997 Handover.* Berkeley: Institute of East Asian Studies, University of California Berkeley, pp. 1–49.

Ma, N. (2007). *Political Development in Hong Kong: State, Political Society, and Civil Society.* Hong Kong: Hong Kong University Press.

Madokoro, L. (2012). Borders transformed: Sovereign concerns, population movements and the making of territorial frontiers in Hong Kong, 1949–1967. *Journal of Refugee Studies*, 25(3), 407–427.

Mark, C. (2017). *The Everyday Cold War: Britain and China, 1952–1972.* London: Bloomsbury Academic.

Mark, C. (2004). *Hong Kong and the Cold War: Anglo–American Relations, 1949–1957.* Oxford: Clarendon Press.

Mark, C. (2007). The "problem of people": British colonials, Cold War powers, and the Chinese refugees in Hong Kong, 1949–62. *Modern Asian Studies*, 41 (6), pp. 1145–1181.

Mathews, G. (1997). Heunggongyahn: On the past, present, and future of Hong Kong identity. *Bulletin of Concerned Asian Scholars*, 29(3), 3–13.

Mathews, G., T.-L. Lui, and E. K. Ma. (2008). *Hong Kong, China: Learning to Belong to a Nation.* London: Routledge.

Mei, J. (1979). Socioeconomic origins of emigration: Guangdong to California, 1850–1882. *Modern China*, 5(4), 463–501.

Meyer, D. R. (2000). *Hong Kong as a Global Metropolis.* Cambridge: Cambridge University Press.

Miners, N. J. (2006). Building the Kowloon–Canton–Hankow Railway. *Journal of the Hong Kong Branch of the Royal Asiatic Society*, 46, 5–24.

Miners, N. J. (1987). *Hong Kong under Imperial Rule, 1912–1941.* Hong Kong: Oxford University Press.

Munn, C. (2001). *Anglo-China: Chinese People and British Rule in Hong Kong, 1841–1880*. Richmond: Curzon.

Munn, C. (1997). The Chusan episode: Britain's occupation of a Chinese island, 1840–46. *Journal of Imperial and Commonwealth History*, 25(1), 82–112.

Munn, C. (2000). The Hong Kong opium revenue, 1845–1885. In T. Brook and B. T. Wakabayashi, eds., *Opium Regimes: China, Britain, and Japan, 1839–1952*. Berkeley: University of California Press, pp. 105–126.

Ng, P. Y. C., and H. D. R. Baker (1983). *New Peace County: A Chinese Gazetteer of the Hong Kong Region*. Hong Kong: Hong Kong University Press.

Ng Lun, N. (1984). *Interactions of East and West: Development of Public Education in Early Hong Kong*. Hong Kong: Chinese University Press.

Ngo, T. (1999). Industrial history and the artifice of *laissez-faire* colonialism. In T. Ngo, ed., *Hong Kong's History: State and Society under Colonial Rule*. London: Routledge, pp. 119–140.

Peckham, R. (2016). *Epidemics in Modern Asia*. Cambridge: Cambridge University Press.

Pedersen, S. (2001). The maternalist moment in British colonial policy: The controversy over "child slavery" in Hong Kong 1917–1941. *Past and Present*, 171, 161–202.

Pepper, S. (1997). Hong Kong, 1997: East vs. West and the struggle for democratic reform within the Chinese state. *Asian Survey*, 37 (8),683–704.

Pepper, S. (2008). *Keeping Democracy at Bay: Hong Kong and the Challenge of Chinese Political Reform*. Lanham, MD: Rowman & Littlefield.

Peterson, G. (2006). To be or not to be a refugee: The international politics of the Hong Kong refugee crisis, 1949–55. *Journal of Imperial and Commonwealth History*, 36(2), 171–195.

Platt, S. R. (2012). *Autumn in the Heavenly Kingdom: China, the West, and the Epic Story of the Taiping Civil War*. New York: Vintage.

Pomerantz-Zhang, L. (1992). *Wu Tingfang (1842–1922): Reform and Modernization in Modern Chinese History*. Hong Kong: Hong Kong University Press.

Pomfret, D. M. (2008). "Child slavery" in British and French Far-Eastern colonies 1880–1945. *Past and Present*, 201, 175–213.

Sanchez-Sibony, O. (2014). *Red Globalization: The Political Economy of the Soviet Cold War from Stalin to Khrushchev*. Cambridge: Cambridge University Press.

Schenk, C. R. (2001). *Hong Kong as an International Financial Centre: Emergence and Development 1945–65*. London: Routledge.

Scott, I. (1995). Political transformation in Hong Kong: From colony to colony. In R. Y-W. Kwok and A. Y. So, eds., *The Hong Kong–Guangdong Link: Partnership in Flux*. Armonk, NY: M. E. Sharpe, pp. 189–223.

Sinn, E. (1994). Chinese patriarchy and the protection of women in 19th-century Hong Kong. In M. Jaschok and S. Miers, eds., *Women and Chinese Patriarchy: Submission, Servitude, and Escape*. Hong Kong: Hong Kong University Press, pp. 141–170.

Sinn, E. (1998). Fugitive in paradise: Wang Tao and cultural transformation in late nineteenth century Hong Kong. *Late Imperial China*, 19(1),56–81.

Sinn, E. (1994). *Growing with Hong Kong: The Bank of East Asia, 1919–1994*. Hong Kong: Bank of East Asia.

Sinn, E. (2011). Hong Kong as an in-between place in the Chinese diaspora, 1849–1939. In D. R. Gabaccia and D. Hoerder, eds., *Connecting Seas and Connected Ocean Rims: Indian, Atlantic, and Pacific Oceans and China Seas Migrations from the 1830s to the 1930s*. Leiden: Brill, pp. 225–247.

Sinn, E. (2013). *Pacific Crossing: California Gold, Chinese Migration, and the Making of Hong Kong*. Hong Kong: Hong Kong University Press.

Sinn, E. (1989). *Power and Charity: The Early History of the Tung Wah Hospital, Hong Kong*. Hong Kong: Oxford University Press.

Smart, A. (2006). *The Shek Kip Mei Myth: Squatters, Fires and Colonial Rule in Hong Kong, 1950–1963*. Hong Kong: Hong Kong University Press.

Smith, C. T. (1985). *Chinese Christians: Elites, Middlemen, and the Church in Hong Kong*. Hong Kong: Oxford University Press.

Smith, C. T. (1981). The Chinese Church, labour and elites and the mui tsai question in the 1920s. *Journal of the Hong Kong Branch of the Royal Asiatic Society*, 21, 91–113.

Snow, P. (2003). *The Fall of Hong Kong: Britain, China, and the Japanese Occupation*. New Haven, CT: Yale University Press.

So, A. Y. (1999). *Hong Kong's Embattled Democracy: A Societal Analysis*. Baltimore, MD: Johns Hopkins University Press.

Sung, Y. (1991). *The China–Hong Kong Connection: The Key to China's Open-Door Policy*. Cambridge: Cambridge University Press.

Tang, J. T. H. (1992). *Britain's Encounter with Revolutionary China*. London: Macmillan.

Ting, J. S. P. (1990). Native Chinese peace officers in British Hong Kong, 1841–1861. In E. Sinn, ed., *Between East and West: Aspects of Social and Political Development in Hong Kong*. Hong Kong: Centre of Asian Studies, University of Hong Kong, pp. 147–158.

Tsai, J. *Hong Kong in Chinese History: Community and Social Unrest in the British Colony, 1842–1913*. New York: Columbia University Press, 1993.

Tsang, S. (2006). *The Cold War's Odd Couple: The Unintended Partnership between the Republic of China and the UK, 1950–1958*. London: I. B. Tauris.

Tsang, S. (1988). *Democracy Shelved: Great Britain, China, and Attempts at Constitutional Reform in Hong Kong, 1945–1952*. Hong Kong: Oxford University Press.

Tsang, S. (1997a). *Hong Kong: An Appointment with China*. London: I. B. Tauris.

Tsang, S. (2004). *A Modern History of Hong Kong*. London: I. B. Tauris.

Tsang, S. (1997b). Strategy for survival: The Cold War and Hong Kong's policy towards Kuomintang and Chinese Communist activities in the 1950s. *Journal of Imperial and Commonwealth Studies*, 25(2), pp. 294–317.

Tsang, S. (1994). Target Zhou Enlai: The "Kashmir Princess" incident of 1955. *China Quarterly*, 139, 766–782.

Tucker, N. B. (1994). *Taiwan, Hong Kong, and the United States, 1949–1992*. New York: Twayne.

Veg, S. (2015). Legalistic and Utopian: Hong Kong's Umbrella Movement. *New Left Review*, 92, 55–73.

Veg, S. (2017). The rise of "localism" and civic identity in post-handover Hong Kong: Questioning the Chinese nation-state. *China Quarterly*, 230, 323–347.

Vickers, E. (2003). *In Search of an Identity: The Politics of History as a School Subject in Hong Kong, 1960s–2002*. New York: Routledge.

Vukovich, D. A. (2020). City and a SAR on fire: As if everything and nothing changes. *Critical Asian Studies*, 52(1),1–17.

Wasserstrom, J. (2020). *Vigil: Hong Kong on the Brink*. With contributions by Amy Hawkins. New York: Columbia Global Reports.

Watson, J. L. (1983). Rural society: Hong Kong's New Territories. *China Quarterly*, 95, 480–490.

White, B. ed. (1996). *Hong Kong: Somewhere between Heaven and Earth*. Hong Kong: Oxford University Press.

Whitfield, A. J. (2001). *Hong Kong, Empire and the Anglo–American Alliance at War, 1941–1945*. Hong Kong: Hong Kong University Press.

Williams, M. (2004). Hong Kong and the Pearl River Delta *Qiaoxiang*. *Modern Asian Studies*, 38(2), 257–282.

Wong, J. D. (2017). Between two episodes of social unrest below Lion Rock: From the 1967 riots to the 2014 Umbrella Movement. In M. H. K. Ng and J. D. Wong, eds., *Civil Unrest and Governance in Hong Kong: Law and Order from Historical and Cultural Perspectives*. New York: Routledge.

Wong, S. (1999). Deciding to stay, deciding to move, deciding not to decide. In G. G. Hamilton, ed., *Cosmopolitan Capitalists: Hong Kong and the Chinese Diaspora at the End of the Twentieth Century.* Seattle: University of Washington Press, pp. 13–51.

Wong, S. (1988). *Emigrant Entrepreneurs: Shanghai Industrialists in Hong Kong.* Hong Kong: Oxford University Press.

Wong, W. (2003). Negotiating gender identity: Postcolonialism and Hong Kong Christian women. In E. W. Y. Lee, ed., *Gender and Change in Hong Kong.* Hong Kong: Hong Kong University Press, pp. 151–176.

Wu, H. (1997). The Hong Kong Clock: Public time-telling and political time/space. *Public Culture*, 9(3), 329–354.

Yahuda, M. (1996). *Hong Kong: China's Challenge.* London: Routledge.

Yahuda, M. (1997). Hong Kong: A new beginning for China? In J. M. Brown and R. Foot, eds., *Hong Kong's Transitions, 1842–1997.* London: Macmillan, pp. 192–210.

Yep, R. (2013). Understanding the autonomy of Hong Kong: Looking beyond formal institutions. In R. Yep, ed., *Negotiating Autonomy in Greater China: Hong Kong and Its Sovereign before and after 1997.* Copenhagen: Nordic Institute of Asian Studies, pp. 3–25.

Yew, C. P., and K. Kwong. (2014). Hong Kong identity on the rise. *Asian Survey*, 54(6), 1088–1012.

Yuen, K. (2004). Theorizing the Chinese: The *mui tsai* controversy and constructions of transnational Chineseness in Hong Kong and British Malaya. *New Zealand Journal of Asian Studies*, 6(2), 95–110.

Yuen, S. (2015). Hong Kong after the Umbrella Movement: An uncertain future for "one country two systems." *China Perspectives*, 2015(1), 49–53.

Acknowledgements

Thanks to Ching Kwan Lee for inviting me to contribute to the Global China series; to Lucy Rhymer, Rachel Blaifeder, James Baker, and Priyadharshini Samidurai at Cambridge University Press for guiding this Element into production; and to three reviewers for offering insightful comments. Tim Ko kindly supplied photos from his amazing collection. I am especially grateful to the hundreds of students at the University of Hong Kong who have taken my course on Hong Kong history over the past fifteen years. They have taught me much about what Hong Kong and China mean to them, and patiently endured my reminiscing about life in 1960s and 1970s Hong Kong. One of them, Duanran Feng, read the draft manuscript twice and helped frame some of its arguments.

Cambridge Elements ≡

Global China

Ching Kwan Lee
University of California-Los Angeles

Ching Kwan Lee is a professor of sociology at the University of California-Los Angeles. Her scholarly interests include political sociology, popular protests, labor, development, political economy, comparative ethnography, China, Hong Kong, East Asia and the Global South. She is the author of three multiple award-winning monographs on contemporary China: Gender and the South China Miracle: Two Worlds of Factory Women (1998), Against the Law: Labor Protests in China's Rustbelt and Sunbelt (2007), and The Specter of Global China: Politics, Labor and Foreign Investment in Africa (2017). Her co-edited volumes include Take Back Our Future: an Eventful Sociology of Hong Kong's Umbrella Movement (2019) and The Social Question in the 21st Century: A Global View (2019).

About the Series

The Cambridge Elements series Global China showcases thematic, region- or country-specific studies on China's multifaceted global engagements and impacts. Each title, written by a leading scholar of the subject matter at hand, combines a succinct, comprehensive and up-to-date overview of the debates in the scholarly literature with original analysis and a clear argument. Featuring cutting edge scholarship on arguably one of the most important and controversial developments in the 21st century, the Global China Elements series will advance a new direction of China scholarship that expands China Studies beyond China's territorial boundaries.

Cambridge Elements ≡

Global China

Elements in the series

Printed in the United States
by Baker & Taylor Publisher Services